EDITED BY
SCOTT D
HARRISON

STORIES OF BOYS

LEARNING THROUGH

MAKING MUSIC

ACER Press

First published 2009
by ACER Press, an imprint of
Australian Council *for* Educational Research Ltd
19 Prospect Hill Road, Camberwell
Victoria, 3124, Australia

www.acerpress.com.au
sales@acer.edu.au

Edited by Renée Otmar, Otmar Miller Consultancy, Melbourne
Cover design by Mason Design
Text design based on design by Kerry Cooke, eggplant communications
Typeset by Mason Design
Printed in Australia by Ligare
Cover image: Bill Reitzel/Digital Vision/Getty Images

National Library of Australia Cataloguing-in-Publication data:

Title:	Male voices : stories of boys learning through making music / edited by Scott D Harrison.
ISBN:	9780864319524 (pbk.)
Notes:	Bibliography.
Subjects:	Gender identity in music.
	Music–Study and teaching–Australia.
	Boys–Australia–Attitudes.
	Masculinity–Australia.
Other Authors/Contributors:	
	Harrison, Scott D. (Scott David), 1962-
Dewey Number:	780.8351

PEFC/21-31-17

PEFC is committed to sustainable forest management through third party forest
certification. For more information go to www.pefc.org

Foreword

From the earliest time I can remember, singing has been second nature to me, like breathing. I did not while away my childhood in the backyard, kicking a footy or learning how to be the next Don Bradman; I was inside, playing my favourite records, running to the piano and creating shows with movement and costumes that kept our entire family, as well as the neighbours it seems, entertained and amused. And even though my father was a mechanic and my brother a plumber, music in our household was a way of life. My mother was a fine pianist and singer, and we were encouraged to follow our individual passions. I am forever grateful to my family for allowing me to indulge in my childhood passions and find my own way to express myself.

Some of my earliest teenage music experiences before attending Melbourne High School, were in fact playing in a pipe band; a strange and ancient ensemble of sorts, I know. But this experience, coupled with hours of music making at an all-boys school, not only gave me a strong sense of community and opportunity for male bonding of sorts, it also showed me how a positive image of men could be nurtured in many ways by the 'elders' of our respective groups of men and boys, who came together several times each week to rehearse and perform our music. Such was the respect and esteem shown by our families and friends for our efforts, that I did indeed feel enormous pride. I was also totally unaware that my passion for music might be thought of in any other way than the norm.

I think that's the key word for me even today: passion. It must have been my natural exuberance and joy in singing and making music that overshadowed any doubt that I might be doing something I was not meant to be, and in my years of wondrous musical exploration at Melbourne High there was nothing else that I could possibly think of pursuing as a career. It felt in many ways the only way I could exist in the world, and how I would be remembered after I left it.

I will be forever grateful to my teachers, mentors and fellow artists, many of them great men, who gave me the musical and vocal skills and confidence to have a career in the music industry for almost 30 years now. They showed me through their passion and love of music that it could be the most honourable and fulfilling way to not only make a living, but also make a contribution to the world we live in. Music has given me the opportunity to leave a legacy, which I know this book will also serve, for many years to come.

JONATHON WELCH

Australian of the Year – Local Hero 2008

ANZAC of the Year, 2008

RMIT Communicator of the Year, 2008

Limelight ABC Music Personality of the Year, 2007

John Campbell MO Award, 2007

St Michael's Medal – Services to Community

Founding Music Director, Choir of Hard Knocks

Contents

Figures

Acknowledgements

I would like to acknowledge the support of Griffith University in the compilation of this volume. In particular, the Dean of Education, Professor Claire Wyatt-Smith, and the Director of Queensland Conservatorium, Professor Peter Roennfeldt, are deserving of mention for their financial contribution and moral support.

To my faithful research assistants, Rachael Dwyer, Paul Faughey and Jessica O'Bryan: this volume would not have been possible without your wisdom, patience, advice and attention to detail. I am indebted to you.

The contributors to this volume have willingly and enthusiastically embraced the opportunity to engage with the issues surrounding males and music in Australia. My thanks to Clare Hall, Anita Collins, Anthony Young, Bob Smith, Kirralee Baldock, Danny Spillane, Scott Mason, Paul Holley, Curtis Bayliss, Jeremy Ludowyke, Anne Lierse and Matthew Hickey for their enthusiasm, goodwill, humour, scholarship and great ideas.

Finally, to the men and boys, named and unnamed, who feature in these pages: your stories are rich and challenging. Thanks for sharing them with us.

SCOTT D. HARRISON

Source acknowledgements

The authors and publisher wish to thank the following for permission to reproduce extracts from their copyrighted works:

Dennis O'Keeffe (p. 5); Billy Brownless, *Billy's Book for Blokes*, Allen & Unwin, Crows Nest, 2008 (pp. 7, 8, 10); Richard Letts (pp. 10–11); W. Martino and M. Pallotta-Chiarolli (p. 9, 13); Hugh Mackay (p. 8); Andrew Parker (p. 13).

Figure 1.1 (p. 11) – photo – Shutterstock.
Figure 5.1 (p. 72) – Reproduced with permission of Noel Ancell, Artistic Director of the Australian Boys Choral Institute.
Figure 8.1 (p. 115) – Reproduced with permission of Tom Corbett, Willow Software.
Figure 10.1 (p. 138) – Reproduced with permission of Melbourne High School.
Figure 10.2 (p. 145) – Reproduced with permission of Melbourne High School.
Figure 10.3 (p. 149) – Reproduced with permission of Melbourne High School.
Figure 10.4 (p. 150) – Reproduced with permission of Melbourne High School.
Figure 10.5 (p. 151) – Reproduced with permission of Melbourne High School.
Figure 10.6 (p. 151) – Reproduced with permission of Melbourne High School.

While every effort has been made to trace and acknowledge copyright owners of material used in this book, there may be some omissions. Any such omissions brought to the publisher's attention, will be corrected in the next printing of the book.

About the authors

Kirralee Baldock

Kirralee Baldock is a music teacher at Glossop High School, South Australia. In 2007, she won a National Teaching Excellence Award for her work in 'transforming music at Glossop from being an energetic embarrassment, to an icon of the highest quality'. As well as developing a highly praised and much-travelled school band, The Glossop Groovers, Kirralee has implemented a Boys Business music program for disengaged students. Its widespread success led to an invitation to present her approach at the 2006 International Middle Years Conference. Kirralee also coordinates 22 primary schools each year for the Riverland and Mallee Primary Schools Music Festival Choir. Kirralee has been teaching for eight years.

Curtis Bayliss

Melbourne tenor Curtis Bayliss is a graduate of the Faculty of Music at The University of Melbourne. Curtis is also a musicology graduate from Monash University. He trained in Librarianship at RMIT and Opera at the Victorian College of the Arts.

From 1997–9, Curtis was Acting Music Director of the Australian Children's Choir and a lecturer in Music and Voice in the School Of Dance at the Victorian College of the Arts, Melbourne. He is currently a voice teacher and Director of Choral Music at Melbourne High School and Lecturer in voice for the Music Theatre course of the Victorian College of the Arts.

As a performer, Curtis has had diverse range of experiences, from classical works with Opera Australia, the Australian Ballet and Victoria State Opera, to rock bands and rock musicals. A founding member of Polyphony (later The Phones), Curtis has been a jazz singer and arranger for vocal groups including Lieder of the Pack, The Rank Sinatras, Gourmet Jazz Big Band and currently BOPeRA. His compositions have been performed by the Melbourne and Playbox Theatre Companies, Whim N' Rhythm of Yale University and many a cappella choral groups in Australia.

Anita Collins

Anita Collins is Convener of Primary and Secondary Music Education at the University of Canberra. She specialises in boys' education, curriculum design, thinking styles and conducting, and has recently published *Bedrock: Foundations in Music*, a text for adult music learners and educators. Her interest in boys' music education came about through her long association with Canberra Grammar School, and was the focus of her masters research at Deakin University.

Clare Hall

Clare Hall is Lecturer in Performing Arts in the Faculty of Education, Monash University. Her background is in music education across all levels. She has a special interest in gender and music, early childhood and music education sociology. Clare is completing a doctoral dissertation in boys' experiences of singing, investigating how young boys negotiate gendered musical identities.

Scott D. Harrison

Scott D. Harrison is Lecturer in Music and Music Education at Griffith University, with teaching and research duties across the Faculty of Education and Queensland Conservatorium. A graduate of Queensland Conservatorium, Scott has experience in teaching singing and music in primary, secondary and tertiary environments. His performance interests and experiences include opera and music theatre, as both singer and musical director. His teaching areas focus on teacher education, research design and gender. Scott maintains contact with school-age activities through Griffith University's Young Conservatorium. He is an internationally recognised scholar in males' involvement in music, a field in which he has published and presented extensively. Scott is the current president of the Australian National Association of Teachers of Singing, and is in demand across the country as an examiner, adjudicator and clinician.

Matthew Hickey

Since 1997, Matthew Hickey has performed around the world as a member and director of Brisbane-based ensemble The Ten Tenors. Highlights include performances at the Eurovision Grand Prix in Germany, recording at Abbey Road Studios in London and working in close collaboration with Oscar-winning composer John Barry and Grammy

Award-winning producer Simon Franglen. Matthew was Executive Producer on The Ten Tenors' platinum-selling album, *Tenology*, and gold-selling album, *Here's to the Heroes*.

In 2001, Matthew was awarded the Centenary Medal by the Commonwealth of Australia for distinguished service to the Australian Music Industry. Matthew holds a degree in political science from the University of Queensland and a Masters of Music from the Queensland University of Technology. He graduated with a degree in law from the Queensland University of Technology in 2008.

Paul Holley

Paul Holley is a graduate of the Queensland Conservatorium of Music, where he studied conducting with Dr John Nickson. He has had extensive experience directing school, church and community choirs. Presently, Paul conducts two ensembles for Brisbane Birralee Voices: The Birralee Blokes – the ABC Classic FM Choir of the Year – and Resonance of Birralee. In addition to these two ensembles, he directs the adult chamber choir, Choral Connection, and he is also Director of Choral Music at Brisbane Girls Grammar School. Paul is dedicated to excellence in choral education, and regularly features as guest conductor/clinician at regional festivals, conferences and music competitions. In 2007, Paul joined the conducting team of Gondwana Voices at their National Summer School. He serves on the committee of the Australian National Choral Association Queensland branch, and in 2007 was awarded a Lord Mayor's Australia Day Achievement Award for his services to the choral community in Brisbane.

Anne Lierse

Dr Anne Lierse is Director of Music at Melbourne High School, where she teaches VCE music, piano and chamber music, and conducts the symphony orchestra. Former positions include director of music at Ivanhoe Girls' Grammar, Blackburn High School, lecturer in Music Education at Monash University and Project Officer (Research) at the Board of Studies. Anne is a member of the Music Council of Australia, vice-president of the Victorian Music Teachers Association and president of the Victorian School Music Action Group, which is responding to the National Review of School Music Education. Anne is actively involved in research, and presents papers and workshops on the effectiveness of music programs, piano pedagogy and the music education of boys.

Jeremy Ludowyke

Jeremy Ludowyke is currently principal of Melbourne High School, having attended the school from 1969 to 1972. He completed the Bachelor of Arts and Diploma of Education programs at La Trobe University, and later a Master of Arts in history. He also completed the Graduate Diploma in Education Policy and Administration at Monash University. Jeremy was principal of Mullauna Secondary College 1990–4 and principal of Princes Hill Secondary College in 1996. He has written on the education of boys, and is an Associate Fellow of the Australian Principals Centre at Melbourne University. He has served on the Ministerial Advisory Committee on Education Employment Training and Youth Affairs and the 1995–6 Gender Equity Task Force, and also on the National Advisory Committee of the National Inquiry into School History and the State Ministerial Reference Group on Gender Education. Jeremy is a board member of the Victorian Schools Innovation Commission and the Youth Research Centre for Melbourne University.

Scott Anthony Mason

Scott Anthony Mason is currently the Director of Performing Arts at All Saints Anglican School, a co-educational Anglican school on the Gold Coast in Queensland. He has previously been director of music at The Southport School (a boys' school) and has taught in the United Kingdom. Scott holds a Bachelor of Music Education from the Queensland Conservatorium of Music and a Masters of Information Technology from Queensland University of Technology. He has taught both music and computing subjects from Years 4 to 12, and he continues to perform professionally on the trumpet in orchestras, brass groups and big bands.

Robert G. Smith

Resident in the Northern Territory since 1986, Dr Bob Smith is a past president of the Australian Society for Music Education and the Northern Territory Institute for Educational Research. Until his 'retirement' in February 2007, he was Music-In-Schools Adviser to the Northern Territory Department of Education, supporting the implementation of the music education curriculum across urban, rural and remote Indigenous Australian regions.

Since his retirement, Bob continues to direct the nationally acclaimed Boys' Business project, which uses music and the arts as vehicles for affirming middle years' boys. He is a regular keynote and workshop presenter interstate in Australia and overseas. His publications include his own evolving series of music education textbooks, which incorporate original music across a range of genres, and academic papers focused on his interests in Pacific and Asian musics, and in gender issues relating to music in education.

Danny Spillane

As Teaching Principal at Kentucky Public School in New South Wales, Danny Spillane has worked tirelessly to bring the same learning experiences to this small rural community as are available to students in larger cities. He has greatly expanded the school's sporting and artistic programs, and has worked to raise literacy and numeracy skills, with 90 per cent of students achieving at or above state benchmarks. Danny has also initiated a music program for 360 students from small, isolated schools to build, and learn to play, their own musical instruments – culminating in performances at the Sydney Opera House and Sydney Entertainment Centre. Danny has been teaching for 25 years.

Anthony Young

Anthony Young teaches and conducts at St Laurence's College in South Brisbane. The school boasts a choral program involving over 150 boys in four choirs. Anthony presently conducts the Brotherhood Choir, a tenor–bass group of 80 singers, and the 24-voice Chamber choir. He has assisted at the Biralee Blokes camp since the group was formed, and has conducted the Australian Boys' Choir changing voice group, 'the Kelly Gang' at their summer camp for the past two years.

Anthony holds the Masters in Music Studies (choral conducting) from the University of Queensland, together with a degree in literature and another in law. He is an experienced choral conductor, having studied with Dr Eduard Bolcovak, Dr John Nickson and Dr Rodney Eichenberger.

At St Laurence, Anthony has enjoyed success in dealing with the male changing voice. He has studied the work of David Jorlett, James Jordan, Kenneth Phillips and Leon Thurmann, and has presented on male changing voice for the Australian National Association for the Teaching of Singing and at the National Conference of the Australian Kodaly Music Education Institute. His latest paper on this issue 'Classroom Strategies for Changing Voice Boys' was published in the *Australian Kodaly Bulletin*.

Introduction

SCOTT D. HARRISON, Griffith University, Queensland

You are probably reading this because you have an interest in the relationship of males with music in Australia. Perhaps you are a teacher, a parent or a school manager. It may be that you are a guy just like those described in these pages. Regardless of your perspective, this book is filled with stories of boys and men participating in the creation of music.

This book offers you a variety of viewpoints. There are academics who position the study of male engagement in music throughout the life cycle, while teachers in private and state schools across the country offer their views alongside those of professional musicians.

The book is structured in three parts:

- The first four chapters lay the foundations, providing overall perspectives of male engagement in music, largely from the academic viewpoint.
- The following six chapters provide practical examples of school processes and activities, based on a variety of perspectives from in-school practitioners.
- The final two chapters examine music beyond schools, in a community organisation and in the profession, respectively.

Chapter 1 describes the study of Australian males' engagement with music. It speaks of the history of masculinity in Australia and of contemporary pressures that inhibit males' involvement with music.

In Chapter 2, Clare Hall presents inspirational stories of boys who love to sing. These stories are provocative examples of young boys' resistance, leading to disruption of the dominant social discourses that inhibit Australian males from engaging in 'feminine' pursuits, such as choral singing. These insights aim to illustrate the power of singing in the lives of young males.

Anita Collins (Chapter 3) provides a model describing the delicate and interconnected environment required in order to maintain boys' engagement in their musical activities. It highlights the messages and

1

experiences that affect that environment, and provides suggestions for how to evaluate and improve the school music program for boys.

In Chapter 4, the experiences of adolescents are heard through the voices of men reflecting on their experiences of music at school and the deterrents they encountered. It also offers suggestions to assist in breaking down the stereotypical barriers from home, school and societal perspectives. As such, it presents both academic research and practical ideas for parents, schools and teachers to assist in addressing the lack of participation by males.

Anthony Young brings us the story of practical, voice-based performance activities, integrated into solid curriculum learning, with efficient use of music technology and instruments, including drum kit, keyboard and guitar. In Chapter 5, Anthony also touches on the manner in which voice change is managed in this environment, through accepted vocal pedagogical practice, and indicates the comprehensive musical involvement that students in this environment experience.

In Chapter 6, the author of *Boys' Business*, Bob Smith, brings tales from the Northern Territory, a focus on individual learners and a movement away from the tendency to 'pigeonhole' learners. His experiences in the 'top end' are rich and compulsory reading for those who wish to embrace individuality in their engagement with music.

Chapter 7 provides an example of the practical extension of the work of Bob Smith in a school in South Australia, provided by Kirralee Baldock. Kirralee is a winner of the National Excellence in Teaching award and provides readers with some specific strategies for students and handy hints for teaching both boys and girls.

Technology has been the domain of males in education and the broader community. In Chapter 8, Scott Mason examines the experiences of students engaging with technology in co-educational and single-sex school environments, seeking to provide strategies for the equitable engagement of students of both sexes in the technology driven, music education environment.

Chapter 9 focuses on boys in rural New South Wales. It describes how Danny Spillane uses marimbas and other instruments to bring about change in academic performance and school attendance. Danny also brings a principal's perspective to the book, demonstrating the value of leadership in engaging boys in the arts.

In Chapter 10, aspects of the delivery of music education at Melbourne High School in Victoria, particularly in relation to its unique singing program, are presented. Jeremy Ludowyke explores the capacity of a singing program to create an affirming school culture that is capable of inspiring creativity, camaraderie and risk taking, with an emphasis on the importance of school leadership. Anne Lierse discusses her role in developing a comprehensive music program in which singing is an essential element. Practitioner Curtis Bayliss discusses perspectives on the development and teaching of musical appreciation and participation through its singing program at Melbourne High School.

Chapter 11 tells the story of the Birralee Blokes from their beginnings, their growth as an ensemble and their success in Australia, and more recently in the international arena. Through the voices of administrators, parents, audience members and the musical director, the philosophy, the pedagogy, the process and the performance experience are shared.

The Ten Tenors are unashamedly Australian, and are not afraid to perform with power, conviction and humour. As such, they present a strong role model for young men in growing up in Australia. In Chapter 12, members of the ensemble tell their story from the perspectives of singers, managers, artistic personnel and fans, with the intention of providing a successful commercial example of how men can sing in Australian culture.

These pages are filled with stories about people, about relationships. There are tales about individual risk takers. There are structures and policies presented for consideration. There are gripping yarns and tall tales. In the final analysis, these 10 vignettes focus on what makes a difference in the lives of Australian men and their music making.

1 | Aussie blokes and music

SCOTT D. HARRISON, Griffith University, Queensland

What comes to mind when we think of men and music in Australia? Do we picture a sweat-stained Jimmy Barnes belting out 'Working Class Man', Richard Tognetti carving up the Bach Violin Concerto in A minor or perhaps a dapper Peter Allen at the piano, singing his unofficial national anthem, 'I Still Call Australia Home'? Maybe it's an anthem of a different kind: Slim Dusty's 'A Pub With No Beer' or Yothu Yindi's 'Treaty'? These few examples, from vastly different genres, give some indication of the extent to which participation in music is shaped by context and taste. While there is no one-size-fits-all way to describe the nexus between Australian men and music, as the diverse cases described in this book demonstrate, this chapter endeavours to explore some of the common themes surrounding images of Australian masculinity, from historical and contemporary perspectives. Central questions to be interrogated in this introductory chapter focus on what it is to be a man in Australian society and how this affects men's engagement with music.

What is it to be an Australian male?

They were meant to be heroes, patriarchs, warriors, powerhouses, impenetrable, immovable, unyielding and without emotion.

These words, from award-winning Australian novelist Tim Winton, reflecting an historical view of the Australian male, provide an entrée to the investigation of how masculine identity has been shaped by events of the past. The first Australians were the Indigenous population, who pre-dated European settlement by an estimated 40,000 to 60,000 years. While research is still emerging about masculinity in the pre-European settlement period, a discussion on Australian masculine identity needs to acknowledge Indigenous Australians and their role as the first Australians.

The first European settlers brought to Australia were convicts transported from 1788. Throughout this period, 140,000 males and 25,000 females came to Australia as convicts. The convict was abandoned: robbed of skills, family and friends. While still on the transportation ship, he began to realise that the only person he could trust was himself. Upon disembarkation, the hardship convicts experienced was extreme. The song 'Van Diemen's Land' (also known as 'The Gallant Poachers', first collected in 1893) reveals the convicts' view of the country upon arrival in Tasmania:

> The first day that we landed here upon the fatal shore,
> The settlers came around us, some twenty score or more;
> They ranked us up like horses and they sold us out of hand,
> And they yoked us up to ploughing frames to plough Van Diemen's Land
> > The hovels that we're living in are built of mud and clay,
> With rotten straw for bedding, and to that we daren't say nay.
> They fence us in with raging fire, and we slumber as we can,
> But it keeps away the wolves and tigers upon Van Diemen's Land

Colling's (1992) research into Australian masculinity reveals that, at the time of European settlement, living in Australia was harsh and difficult: the first European men had to adapt to a new, inhospitable landscape, inhumane treatment and appalling living conditions. In 'Waltzing Down the Years', musician Dennis O'Keeffe describes the first European settlers in Tasmania's Port Arthur in this way:

> They who came here in chains, who were lashed while they worked in convict gangs at Port Arthur.
> > They who like many others were driven through starvation or oppression from their home-lands to the shores of this new country, Australia.
> > They, who for a multitude of reasons that hopefully, I or my children will never witness or experience, decided not to harbour grudges or discontent but rather to look to the future.
> > They who embraced this country as their own and said; 'let's get on with it, this is a new land, this is our home.'

In order to 'get on with it', the convict needed to repress any softer emotions that might make him vulnerable to exploitation. Records from the time indicate that there were approximately four men for every woman in the cities, growing to a 20:1 ratio of men to women in the country. The paucity of women contributed to distinctive styles of behaviour by the men, and the concept of mateship began to develop.

Contempt for authority

The convicts were joined by free immigrants from the early 1790s. Migrants arriving after the First Fleet included Italians, Greeks, Malays and other Europeans. The early settlers developed a 'survival frontier mentality', which united against authority. Early European settlers in Australia who took over Aboriginal land had to suppress feelings of pity, fear and compassion, and to value loyalty, reliability, ingenuity, courage, toughness and humour.

The gold rush of the 1850s reinforced competitiveness and distrust of authority. At the height of the gold rush, the Eureka Stockade, which took place in Ballarat, Victoria, enshrined egalitarianism and dissipated any remnants of a class structure. The post-gold rush period saw the emergence of bushrangers like Ned Kelly, Mad Dog Morgan and Ben Hall, who became unlikely role models. Kelly's *Jerilderie Letter* (1879) expounds his view of the conduct of authority figures:

> ... *brutal and cowardly conduct of a parcel of big ugly fat-necked wombat headed big bellied magpie legged narrow hipped splay footed sons of Irish Bailiffs or English landlords which is better known as officers of Justice or Victorian Police who some calls honest gentlemen* ...

The two world wars brought the opportunity to be a hero. Australian men were suited to war, with their suppression of tender emotions and their sense of loyalty to one another. The events of World War I, including the battles at Pozières and Gallipoli, galvanised this attitude. British military men who served with Australian troops were known to comment on this concept of loyalty. One such reference came from Lieutenant-General Adrian Carton de Wiart who made these remarks in relation to Australian soldiers:

> *The Australians, to my mind, were the most aggressive and managed to keep their form despite their questionable discipline. Out of the line they were undoubtedly difficult to handle, but once in it they loved a fight. They were a curious mixture of toughness and sentimentality.*

http://sthweb.bu.edu/archives/index.php?option=
com_awiki&view=mediawiki&article=Portal:Military_of_Australia/Quotes

In the 1960s and early 1970s, the Vietnam War exposed the myth of heroics while simultaneously embodying anti-authority, particularly as Australia withdrew from the conflict. Women became more actively involved in the workforce, thus blurring traditionally established gender roles. Australian songs from the time also embody the lack of trust in authority and emphasis on mateship. Graham (Shirley) Strachan, lead singer of the 1970s band Skyhooks, was described as a loud-mouthed larrikin with a passion for surfing, womanising and practical jokes. Repertoire such as 'Why Don't You All Get F*****' and 'All My Friends Are Getting Married' captured aspects of anti-authority and patriarchy. Hitherto unchallenged concepts enshrined within patriarchal society were questioned through the rise of the feminist movement, and male identity itself came under scrutiny.

A more culturally diverse Australia emerged with the abolition of the White Australia Policy in 1972, when Australia became home to immigrants from more than 150 countries. This diversity provides some challenges in defining the typical Australian male. Australian media representations of males tend towards two-dimensional roles that reinforce the stereotypes of the White (albeit tanned), beer-drinking, sport-watching, beach bum. This representation, along with notions of the wide brown land, the unusual wildlife and the 'throw a shrimp on the barbie' image, is promoted as our identity within Australia and to other parts of the world. A constant theme from convict times to the present has been that of mateship.

Mateship

> The greatest pleasure I have ever known is when my eyes meet the eyes of a mate over the top of two foaming glasses of beer. (Henry Lawson)

Mateship is promoted as one way in which Australian masculinity is homogenised. McLean (1995, p.85) encapsulates the role of mateship in establishing the typical Australian male:

> Male camaraderie or 'mateship' is founded on sharing the rituals of masculine identity. The exclusion of women is an integral aspect, and many of these rituals turn out to be destructive or oppressive. Binge drinking, gambling and violent sports are obvious examples.

The binge drinking, gambling and violent sports to which McLean refers are obvious examples of how mateship is enacted. In the 2008 publication *Billy's Book for Blokes*, former Geelong footballer and media personality Billy Brownless sums it up in this way:

> I'm a bloke. I like a beer and a bet. I love my footy. I love the Darl and my kids. I'm like just about every other bloke in this country. (p. 1)

Brownless is taking a humorous view, but there is a grain of truth in his writing. One of the reasons for projecting this image is that Brownless is concerned that this type of masculinity is becoming extinct. He writes:

... we are an endangered species, us blokes. That's right, there's this other species of man they've dubbed the sensitive new age guy. He is ruining it for all of us with his political correctness, snappy dress sense and use of facial creams.

Former Labor Party leader Mark Latham concurs. In *A Conga Line of Suckholes* (2006), he laments the loss of the Australian language's 'larrikin' character. He says:

One of the saddest things I have seen in my lifetime has been the decline in Australian male culture: the loss of our larrikin language and values ... Australian mates and good blokes have been replaced by nervous wrecks, metrosexual knobs and tossbags.

Social commentator Hugh Mackay (2005) disagrees, suggesting that the metrosexual 'came and went in a cloud of aftershave'. Mackay posits that an alternative type of Australian male has developed:

New Bloke has emerged: comfortable both with his masculinity (unlike the pathetic and doomed SNAG, invented then soon despised by women), and with the new meanings of female liberation. The old-fashioned larrikin is not far beneath the surface, but the New Bloke knows that male chauvinism was only ever a panicked, defensive rear-guard attempt to slow the process of men's ultimate acceptance of women as true equals. (n.p.)

Singleton (2005) also questions whether the old-fashioned Aussie bloke (whom he describes as 'the fella clutching the beer at the barbie, gut hanging over his shorts') is an endangered species. He concurs with Mackay that the existence of the so-called 'new man' is often anecdotal. Singleton claims that the traditional Aussie male, far from being extinct, may have reinvented himself under the guise of new masculinity. The stereotypical Australian man may not exist in the purest sense, but the image promoted through sport and the media gives some strength to the perception that Australian males are beer-swilling, sports-loving chauvinists.

Rugby League writer and presenter Matthew Johns (2004) does little to dispel this image when he introduces us to his alter-ego, Reg Reagan:

Reg Reagan typifies some uniquely Australian values: he loves a beer or twenty, is a self-confessed ladies' man, practises an extreme form of on-field violence, sticks by his mates ...

Johns goes on to describe Reagan's attributes as liking to 'score tries, sink piss and bang birds'. Reagan's favourite meal is lamb chops, chips, a can of beer and a smoke.

The love of alcohol has been another constant theme; one that is enshrined in songs such as 'A Pub With No Beer', in which the absence of alcohol causes Billy the blacksmith to go home sober and break down. This song, so much a part of Australian culture, also refers to the woman being 'in the kitchen' when Billy comes home sober for the first time in his life! Such images can reinforce the unhealthy stereotypical images of the male at the pub relying on alcohol and his mates for company, while the woman stays at home cooking, cleaning and child-rearing.

A similar alcohol-related theme is evident in the iconic Men at Work song, 'Down Under', in which the references include excessive consumption of beer which subsequently causes men to 'chunder'. At the time of writing, binge drinking on this scale is in the public eye, especially in its connection with sport and high-profile sportspeople as male role models.

The association of alcohol consumption with masculinity finds support in the research literature, particularly in relation to sport, as Martino and Pallotta-Chiarolli (2001, p. 6) found:

You're supposed to go to the footy, you're supposed to drink a six-pack every week and you're supposed to watch action movies over and over again. I don't like football, I don't like cricket and I can cook. All that probably makes me, in society's view, not that flash. There is a real male stereotype out there for football watchers and beer-swilling hillbillies, but I think you can't really put a definition onto manhood. I think being a man is whatever you want it to be (Andrew, aged 16).

Gender-role rigidity

Andrew's assertion above that it is not possible to define masculinity is fair enough: many men do not fit the stereotype. The price for being 'whatever you want to be' can, however, be a high one. The stereotypical Australian male is maintained by the existence of male gender-role rigidity: the restriction of gender-role development and expression, brought about through a lack of ability for males to experience femininity as much as females experience masculinity. Pollack (1999) refers to gender-role rigidity as affecting the way boys shy away from expressing signs of neediness, dependence, sadness or vulnerability. If unspoken limits of masculinity are transgressed or rules broken, then the full fury of male condemnation rapidly descends on the guilty party. Probably the most crucial way in which this occurs is through the taboo against homosexuality. Homophobia becomes a powerful weapon for preventing any challenge to the accepted masculine ways of being.

The 'norm' is typically defined in the research literature as 'hegemonic masculinity', which refers to the dominant and dominating forms of masculinity. The majority of men may not consciously subscribe to this form of masculinity, but it asserts its influence through cultural and institutional practices. Hegemonic masculinity in Australia has an historical basis that continues to be maintained through many avenues. Brownless (2008, p. 145) captured these historical and contemporary trends in his statement about mateship:

> Mateship is entrenched in this country's history. Our boys fighting at Gallipoli and enduring the hardships at Changi prisoner of war camp personify this concept of mateship ... whenever you are together; no mate is immune from having shit hung on him. Everyone there is expected to play an active part in bagging the crap out of each other for the majority of the time you're together.

'Bagging' or 'hanging shit' is one of the ways in which mates feel forced to subscribe to the hegemonic view of masculinity. While the 'larrikin' does this in a fun way, it can seriously restrict the types of behaviours with which Australian men feel comfortable, including music making.

To sum up, several themes defining Australian masculinity have become apparent throughout the discussion thus far. Contempt for authority, participation in sport, love of beer and the resultant gender-role rigidity contribute to the construction of the Australian male identity, as depicted in Figure 1.1. There are, of course, many other contributing factors that help to define the Australian male, including patriarchy, feminist thought, the dominance of sport in media coverage and the avoidance of femininity. The reference list at the end of this chapter points readers to publications in which these factors are pursued in greater detail. 'Music Versus Sport: What's the score?' (Harrison, 2003) and *Masculinities and Music* (Harrison, 2008) might be of particular interest.

Do Australian men engage in music?

> Australians perform and listen to a plethora of musical styles. Participation is numerically greatest in styles promoted by the international popular music industry – e.g. rock music, hip hop, dance/electronica. Other styles include country music, including a stream identified with indigenous musicians; classical music in all its forms; jazz; Australian folk and bush music derived from Anglo-Celtic folk styles; ethnic styles, especially but not exclusively those associated with the cultures of immigrants, including 'world music'; traditional indigenous musics; fusion musics that experiment with

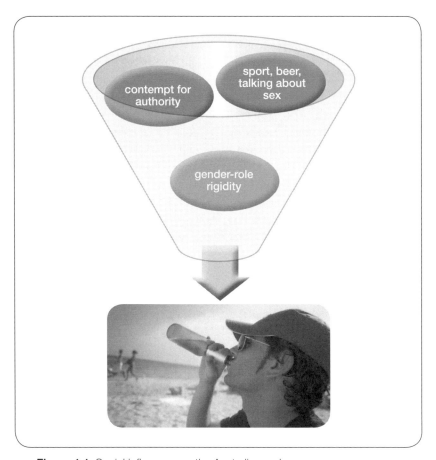

Figure 1.1: Social influences on the Australian male

couplings of any of the above; experimental music/computer-generated music/multimedia. (Letts, 2003, p. 3)

There is little doubt that Australian men and boys engage with music and have done since European settlement. There is a long history of men performing in the variety of styles described by Letts (2003) and evidenced in the examples cited at the beginning of this chapter. There is, however, a disjunct between the level of participation in the broader population and the engagement of boys in school music.

Boys and music in schools

In 'Real Men Don't Sing' (Harrison, 2001), I established that under certain circumstances, Australian men do participate in music, yet familiar trends are still apparent: almost no boys in co-educational schools are singing, and small numbers of boys are playing the flute and other so-called 'feminine' instruments. There is an historical perspective to this phenomenon: 40 years ago, Bartle (1968, p.188) commented that 'a cause of some concern is the frequency in co-educational Australian schools of choirs of girls only'. At least half of his 474-school sample was not using the voices of the senior boys to any significant extent. In more recent research undertaken into gender balance in school choirs in Australia, statistics indicate that in primary schools, 80 per cent of the singing is done by girls, increasing to 90 per cent in secondary schools. Solo singing also attracts a high proportion of females: over 90 per cent of students enrolled in individual voice tuition are female (Harrison 2003, 2007). Pickering and Repacholi (2001, p. 642), also working in Australia, noted that:

> The perceived risk associated with playing ... a gender-inappropriate instrument [on a survey] was probably much greater for the boys than for the girls. Boys in particular could benefit from exposure to multiple examples of a counter-stereotyped behaviour.

Counter-stereotypical behaviour is one strategy that has been explored throughout the case studies in the remainder of this book, but this quote indicates that gender-role rigidity continues to be a problem for young men wishing to engage in the arts. As Epstein, Elwood, Hey and Maw (1998) noted: homophobic abuse is levelled at boys who 'dislike rough and tumble games ... preferring gentler pursuits' (p. 103). Gentler pursuits probably include the arts. Males can be subjected to ridicule, bullying and suspicion about their sexuality at school when they are involved in certain musical activities. It is apparent that degrees of masculinity and femininity attributed to boys are based partly on music participation.

I recently conducted some interviews to ascertain the extent to which homophobic abuse is a reality for boys in schools (Harrison, 2008). These interviews were undertaken with men who reflected on their experiences of school music. One of the participants, Dean, contemplated what happened when he expressed a desire to dance and sing, consequently risking his masculine status:

> I decided to become a Music Theatre performer – to rise above the other dickhead boys at school. I also secretly loved to dance – something which I think was evident when I was very little but my parents didn't encourage it because of its association with homosexuality.

This response would appear to reinforce the views of Lehne (1992), who describes involvement in arts (as singer, dancer, musician, artist, actor) as being 'sissy' work. 'Sissy' work is devalued by rewarding success in sports and traditionally masculine academic areas such as mathematics and sciences, while marginalising artistic activity. The status of music as a subject is discussed in more detail in Chapter 4, but the compulsory nature of participation in sport and its association with the construction of masculinity is worthy of discussion here. Plummer (1999) suggests that an Australian boy who doesn't play sport, or avoids sports, is considered a 'poofter'. Parker's (1996) research also supports this view:

> ... poofs can't do anything can they ... I mean, y'know ... I mean, a person who is a sort of a poof is a sort of a woman ... I mean girl trying to catch a rock hard ball, kind of thing, has got about the same chance as a poof catching it ... so that's why you call them a poof ...

The research of Martino and Pallotta-Chiarolli (2001, p. 9) found explicit examples of how this behaviour is realised in the experiences of boys:

> You have to be tough, you have to swear, be rude to girls, you have to have a deep voice because if you don't you'll get hassled. They used to hassle me because of my higher voice, calling me gay. It's just that everyone's voice matured before mine. (Jacob, aged 15)

In my own research (Harrison, 2008), Dean didn't experience name-calling of this type, but his experience of music and sport was still damaging:

> In primary school, I didn't remember getting any crap for doing music, but think it had a profound effect on how I related to the other boys as all of them were playing football while I was playing the violin. It created a real divide between me and the other guys which I think still remains with me now in terms of how I relate to other guys.

Dean's bullying was one of isolation and the social rejection affected his relationships for many years. In Dean's case, simple rescheduling of the times for football and music may have resolved some of his issues.

Another participant, Peter, took a somewhat different approach. He took up sport and this gave him identity 'capital': an opportunity to improve status. There is a hierarchy within sport, with football (rugby league, rugby union or Australian rules football) ranked highest. Sporting status is judged on participation, team spirit and perceived toughness of the sport, so Peter chose well:

> I was good at cricket and rugby league so I had it all covered. I also knew how to look after myself if anyone gave me shit.

Peter was fortunate. He was good at a high-status sport; he was resilient and he could look after himself. Life could easily have dealt him a different hand, as it has for many Australian males.

Conclusion

Men have to contend with the historical construct of masculinity (particularly since European settlement); a construct that celebrates fearlessness, hardship and contempt for authority. In contemporary Australia, the emphasis on valuing men who play sport, drink alcohol and display gender-role rigidity has resulted in a society in which engagement in music, particularly in schools, is inhibited.

Yet, it is not all 'doom and gloom' for Australian males and their involvement in music.

Jimmy Barnes is just one of many men who have been 'working hard to make a living' in music, as have the other men cited earlier in this chapter. The problem is neither universal nor insurmountable. Challenging the authenticity of the stereotypical image is the first step. By presenting counter-stereotypical images, allowing for plurality in musical and non-musical activities and promoting tolerance for difference, men can engage in whatever music they like, at school and beyond. The chapters that follow provide examples of ways in which boys and men have triumphed in their musical endeavours. These examples demonstrate the processes through which men can be fulfilled in their music making.

References

Bartle, G. (1968). *Music in Australian Schools*, Melbourne: Australian Council for Education, Wilke and Company.

Brownless, A.W. (2008). *Billy's Book for Blokes*, Sydney: Allen & Unwin.

Colling, T. (1992). *Beyond Mateship: Understanding Australian men*, Sydney: Simon and Schuster.

Epstein, D., Elwood, J., Hey, V., & Maw, J. (eds) (1998). *Failing Boys: Issues in gender and achievement*, Buckingham: Open University Press.

Harrison, S.D. (2001). Real Men Don't Sing, *Australian Voice*, *11*, pp. 31–6.

Harrison, S.D. (2003). Music Versus Sport: What's the score, *Australian Journal of Music Education*, *1*, pp. 10–15.

Harrison, S.D. (2007). Where Have the Boys Gone? The perennial problem of gendered participation in music, *British Journal of Music Education*, 24(3), pp. 267–80.

Harrison, S.D. (2008). *Masculinities and Music*, Newcastle: Cambridge Scholars Publishing.

Johns, M. (2004). *Reg Reagan: This is my life*, Sydney: Macmillan.

Kelly, N. (1879). *Jerilderie Letter*, Melbourne: State Library of Victoria, http://www.slv.vic.gov.au/collections/treasures/jerilderieletter/jerilderie43.html, accessed 20/03/2008.

Latham, M. (2006). *A Congaline of Suckholes: Mark Latham's book of quotations*, Melbourne: Melbourne University Press.

Lehne, G. (1992). Homophobia Among Men: Supporting and defining the male role, in M. Kimmel and M. Messner (eds), *Men's Lives*, pp. 416–29, Needham Heights, MA: Allyn and Bacon.

Letts, R. (2003). The Effects of Globalisation on Music in Five Contrasting Countries: Report of a research project for the Many Musics program of the International Music Council, Music Council of Australia.

Mackay, H. (2005). *Australia and the World: The Australian paradox*, Canberra: Centre for Policy Development, http://cpd.org.au/article/australia-and-world:-australian-paradox, accessed 1/08/2008.

Martino, W. & Pallotta-Chiarolli, M. (2001). *Boys Stuff: Boys talking about what matters*, Sydney: Allen & Unwin.

McLean, C. (1995). The Costs of Masculinity: Placing men's pain in the context of male power, reproduced in *Gender Equity: A framework for Australian schools*, pp. 85–8. Canberra: MCEETYA.

Parker, A. (1996). The Construction of Masculinity within Boys Physical Education, *Gender and Education*, 8(2), pp. 141–57.

Pickering, S. & Repacholi, B. (2001). Modifying Children's Gender-typed Musical Instrument Preferences: The effects of gender and age, *Sex Roles*, 45(9/10), pp. 623–42.

Plummer, D. (1999). *One of the Boys: Masculinity, homophobia and modern manhood*, New York: Harrington.

Pollack, W. (1999). *Real Boys*, New York: Holt.

Singleton, A. (2005). Fathers: More than breadwinners?, in M. Poole (ed.) *Family: Changing families, changing times,* Sydney: Allen & Unwin.

Winton, T. (1994). The Masculine Mystique, *The Age Good Weekend*, 27 August, pp. 61–7.

2) 'Without music I'd just be another kid': Boys and the choral experience

CLARE HALL, Monash University, Victoria

Singing is at the heart of Thomas's life. His story portrays his deep-felt experience of singing in a boys' choir and how singing informs his understanding of himself and his world. Thomas's experience counters the popular discourse that frames singing, particularly choral singing, as troublesome for emerging masculinities. This chapter illustrates the complexities of boys' gendered musical identities by presenting the unique musical pathway that has enabled Thomas to reject the notion that 'boys don't sing'.

Investigating boys' singing

Without doubt, music education is not a negative experience for all boys, because males continue to dominate many fields. While I am concerned about a growing perception that 'boys who sing are special, while girls who sing are ordinary' (O'Toole, 1998, p. 9), I do believe the impoverished state of male participation in singing in Australia warrants particular attention. The predominance of females' singing in many English-speaking cultures is a highly discussed area of research (Gates, 1989; Green, 1997). Choral singing is shown to be one of the most commonly avoided musical activities of boys (Adler & Harrison, 2004). Indeed, it is not a new issue that Australian boys' participation in singing inside and outside of school is relatively marginal at any age (Australian Bureau of Statistics, 2000, 2003, 2006; Bartle, 1968).

Boys' experiences of singing have been problematised as complex and often overlapping issues associated with masculine identity, the voice change and vocal pedagogy (Adler, 1999; Bennetts, 2008; Cooksey, 1999; Goetze, Cooper & Brown, 1990; Hall, 2005; Koza, 1994; Welch, Sargeant & White, 1997). This body of knowledge brings to the foreground the social and cultural dimensions involved in becoming a singer and learning to sing: family, peers, teachers, school, pedagogy, ethnicity, gender and age. Central to the current debates about the 'missing males' in singing (Koza, 1993) is boys' avoidance of 'feminine' behaviours, such as singing high, singing in a choir and singing in school, in favour of more 'masculine' ways of being (Adler, 2002; Hall, 2003; Harrison, 2003a). Extant historical research supports how the feminine 'genderedness' (Dame, 1994) of vocal music has affected the participation of boys and men in singing in Western cultures for centuries (Green, 1997; Koza, 1993; McClary, 1991; Dunn & Jones, 1994). Males employing the use of a higher vocal register shared with females can represent one of the greatest musical gender contraventions for males.

> When boys and girls do take up alternative musical practices, they are challenging conventional gender delineations in what may be a courageous gesture that contravenes the stereotyping assumptions of a wider, powerful discourse. (Green, 1997, p. 187)

The fear of performing 'musical transvestism' (Green, 1993) results in many boys making the decision not to sing, which is typically understood as a problem that occurs during the transition from primary to secondary school, when peer relations are thought to be most critical in emerging identities. However, there is an abundance of research that illustrates the construction of gender boundaries in early childhood and primary school years, and the impact this has on children's beliefs, actions and learning (Blaise, 2005; Connolly, 2004; Skelton, 2001; Epstein, Kehily, Mac an Ghail & Redman, 2001). It would be illogical to presume that gender issues are any less important in the musical lives of young children than they are for adolescents; therefore, further investigation is needed into the construction of masculinities and femininities in early childhood music, as little research exists in this area.

The picture of boys' participation in singing is further complicated by the fact that many boys do engage in various kinds of singing, many schools do not have problems retaining boys in their choirs, many boys do continue singing beyond primary school and many do not experience the voice change as a deterrent. We know a little about the resources boys use to make singing 'safe' (Adler, 2002; Phillips, 2003), such as sporty dispositions (Harrison, 2003b) and selecting single-sex (Smith, 2001) or outside-of-school vocal groups (Hall, 2007). These inquiries have generated interest in boys' singing; however, only a handful of English-language studies have specifically investigated the gendered nature of the boy voice (Adler, 2002; Ashley, 2006; Austern, 1994; Borgerding, 2006; Hall, forthcoming; Shapiro, 1994; Welch & Howard, 2002).

Because the experience of singing differs between individuals and contexts, further research is required to understand the depth of the issues with boys' singing. While statistical trends shed light on patterns of participation, such generalisations leave exceptions to the rule and the significance of context unexplained. I consider it important to remain critical about what we mean by 'boys' experiences', 'boys' educational needs', 'role models for boys', for example – even 'boys' singing'. I am conscious of not generalising 'boys' as an homogeneous group with similar experiences in life merely because of their gender. Which boys are we talking about? Age, socio-economic background, cultural background, schooling, peer and family relations, affect one's experience of life and music. These axes of difference intersect to make up the individual, and no two people will have the same intersections. Therefore, in order to understand young people's *experience* of music, I consider it important to examine the individual in depth.

Boys' stories of singing

My investigation seeks to provide a nuanced examination of masculinity and music by illustrating the complex relationship between boys' singing and their gendered identities. I have conducted a sociological study of boy choristers aged 8–13 years who volunteered to share their stories. They came from a non-religious male choral organisation in Australia, renowned for excellence in music education and attracting boys and men who are passionate about singing. Their narratives provide insights into what enables some boys to challenge gender norms and subvert the notion that singing is symbolically 'feminine'. These insights offer potential lessons in how to improve boys' participation in singing.

The following section introduces Thomas[1], a 13-year-old chorister who said, 'without me knowing music I'd just be another kid'. His 'counter story' contrasts the themes reported in boys' singing research: he loves singing in choir, he kept singing through the transition from primary to secondary school, he does not think singing is girly and is aware that others do, but has never considered giving up. He disregards the negative consequences he has suffered from his peers because of his singing, and is not concerned about his voice changing. Singing in choir influences how he understands himself and others around him; it is clearly a powerful experience.

As a music teacher, I wonder how Thomas and boys like him have been able to experience singing so profoundly when the majority of their peers do not sing at all. In terms of influencing the students in my class who are not so sure about the value of singing, it is not as simple as me teaching more effectively or being a better role model. While that is important, what *I do* does not explain the differences among my students, given that they all receive the same teaching from me. Thomas's story shows that he is acutely aware of these differences; that he is going against the 'norm' and that he is aware of the potential costs of this contravention. But more significantly, Thomas sings in choir regardless, and he is proud to do so. What enables Thomas to do what he does, to show such determination and at a young age? I believe my questions are better answered by looking at what students bring *with* them into a given context. Thus, my perspective looks into the individual and out into their world beyond the classroom.

The aim of the next section is to share Thomas's deep-felt experience with singing in choir, what this enables him to understand of himself and his world and how he uses singing as a valuable resource to be the boy he wants to be.

Thomas and his choral experience

Although initially shy, Thomas made his enthusiasm to talk with me clear. I had planned to interview only pre-adolescent boys, but being 13 years old, Thomas requested the chance to participate. I included him, interested to find out why he was so keen. Immediately, I realised how important singing was for him: in his words singing 'is a very major factor in my life. It's quite literally my whole life, the whole thing. Everything else is just a minor detail'. Angela, Thomas's mother, agreed that choir 'is more important than anything else. It's no longer outside school or outside another life, it's the main thing, and school is something that you have to do.' As I got to know Thomas I became increasingly moved by his stories of singing. Such was the emotion in his storytelling that at one point his own eyes welled with tears as he spoke. It is for this reason I have selected Thomas's story to share.

Looking for someone else like him

Thomas positions himself as different from other boys. The time Thomas spends thinking repeatedly features as what he believes sets him apart from others. Angela agrees that he 'thinks a lot. He's always been very thoughtful, very sensitive to other people's moods.' He sets himself high standards and is the kind of student who feels a pressure to deliver.

I used to feel like I was a total loner. I used to think I was weird too because all I did was just walk around thinking about things that didn't even mean anything to me – like exams, for example.

They [girls] all like singing and dancing. Boys are more of a hang out. They're more sporty. I don't know. I really don't know. I was nothing like them, I was like an outcast. I just used to walk around thinking to myself.

I guess you could say I am the tree, okay. I am a tree and all the other boys are the birds. They talk and they do all their stuff while I sit there quietly thinking to myself and hearing other conversations. I might jump in by moving a branch, talking to them and come into the conversation, but just to talk. I do feel lonely sometimes, but otherwise, I'm just the tree that sits there, walks around, does something and listens to everyone else do things. Like, overseer.

Thomas has a highly visual way of explaining his thoughts and is an excellent artist, so I suggested he illustrate his tree analogy (see Figure 2.1). The ears and the eyes on the tree are him listening and seeing everyone around him. The birds are the 'people that like me, ignore me, dislike me'. The roots represent his life, and the two small trees on the world is his hope to find someone else like him. He explains the watering can:

People that like me make me feel overall better – teachers – all the water nourishing me or teaching me, making me better myself – learn and grow. People that like me generally make me feel better.

In another instance, Thomas describes himself as a chameleon, which reflects the importance of adaptability in his story:

I guess I'm kind of a chameleon, though. I turn myself into a person I need according to my surroundings, like if I'm around country kids I would be running around, being more optimistic, stuff like that. It just depends on the surroundings. I do change my moods a lot.

Choir: sanctuary or tonic?

The single-sex choir has been described as a sanctuary for adolescent boys; a place of refuge where they can feel safe to explore 'their most authentic selves without fear of reprisal' (Adler, 2002, p. 269; Phillips, 2003). The general argument here is that boys come into a social space where they can collectively experience an alternative way of 'doing boy' (Swain, 2004). Notwithstanding pedagogical strategies, the safety to participate in a 'feminine' activity is generated by the critical mass or safety in numbers and by seclusion from the female gaze. Alternatively,

Figure 2.1: Thomas's 'I am a tree' illustration

boys' choirs may specialise in perfecting hegemonic masculinity as a way of defining the 'boys-only zone' that is impervious to ridicule.[2] Thomas speaks about the choral space as one that he comes into from the outside world. This image would seem to agree that he, too, considers it a sanctuary. He says:

> … every day I'm longing to come here. And I see that we're all normal kids. There are different people on the outside, there are academic people, there is a different range of thinkers, and there will be the rebels, sporty type people, and the people who don't like school and stuff like that. I can't really categorise them because they are all different in that way but everyone in the world listens to music. They listen to us and I guess we are a part of their society, part of the day until we come to choir again.

Clare (author): It's when you come to choir you see that as going into the inside?

Thomas: Yes.

C: It is somehow separate?

T: Yes, like a double-agent kind of thing!

I am interested in how individual life stories complicate the neatness of the choir-as-sanctuary notion. Thomas implies that he is leading something of a double life by singing in a choir and being a boy. But, as you will see from the following narratives, Thomas's ambivalence towards masculinity and his overt singing at school contradict the idea that he seeks an escape from the gender troubles of his outside life. So, what is the sanctuary he seeks; is he looking for a sanctuary from himself? Thomas consciously uses singing as a resource to help himself feel better, as he says, 'to keep optimistic all the time because, with the things that are going on and me growing up and stuff'. When he is singing he stops thinking and lets it all 'flow out'.

Ultimately singing, I feel, is a way to express yourself even if they don't actually get it, at least it's out in the air – like the audience or whoever is listening – even if they don't get the message at least it's out. You feel a whole relief when it's all out.

I question how his life might be different without the singing experiences he has had:

I think I wouldn't have changed at all. I've had a lot of bottled up feelings through seeing stuff that happened, like happy stuff, sad stuff, things that made me really angry and I guess singing just uncorked the bottle and let it flow out.

Thomas assures me that choir is more about the music than the socialising for him. Angela says that after choir he and his brother are so 'full of it' she has to turn the car radio off from all the singing in the back seat; he has a new energy, it is like she has 'given him a tonic'. He obviously has a very high emotional response to singing and it is this connection Thomas chooses to focus on in our conversations. My observations add another perspective, as I have seen a boy who has a great time socialising with his friends. One might expect stories of fun to be a major factor in boys' motivation to persist with choral singing; however such stories are absent from Thomas's narrative, and I am conscious of him using the interview conversation as an outlet for his emotions at a particular moment in his life. Nonetheless, his focus on the 'tonic affect' of singing emphasises the significance of the music's 'psychic work' for him (Reay, 2002).

Another layer to Thomas's story is that his experience of the choir and what singing means are inextricably connected to what the choir represents to his whole family. This highlights the difficulty in defining what works for one boy and applying that as a 'truth' for other boys. Thomas's brother is also a member of the choir, and Angela participates actively on the parent committee. She describes the choir as providing the social support they have missed since leaving their home overseas a few years ago. There, they experienced 'love in the community', and joining the choir was a 'big bonding step to take' for the whole family. She says 'meeting new people and for us as parents, for me especially, interacting socially … was a good experience overall for all of us.' It was not until the family took a holiday that they realised what a large part of their lives the choir had become, because 'we were not involved with any other sport or any other extracurricular activity, choir was the main thing'. Apart from the new friends the choir has helped them to make, Angela also sees the benefits in smoothing the transition from one country to another.

> … [choir has] been good for them to realise that besides study, they're good at something. To them it's been a big achievement that they've been planning on, so it's been very nice for them to get that confidence and feel that this move, coming to a new country, new place, after leaving everything that was familiar and comfortable, it wasn't a bad thing.

Becoming more himself through music

'Just being another kid' is the antithesis of how Thomas constructs himself, even among his fellow choirboys. Within the choir, he explains, there are those who 'sing for the sake of it' and those like him, who have a real feeling for music.

> T: Singing for me – I guess each piece is a different world that you visit each time. Depending on how you sing it the world changes slightly and you get to see different things and stuff. That changes how you feel. You could sing a really happy song but that can still make you feel melancholy.
>
> C: So singing is about feelings?
>
> T: Yes.
>
> C: Does everybody have the same experience or is this just you?

T: No. I've talked to some of the younger kids – I kind of get the feeling that some of the younger singers think singing is just singing; it's fun, that's it. Only some of them really feel for it. If you're really into a song you just get carried away by it and you don't really sense anything around you. You're really into it and you just keep on going. I've been in this experience once or twice.

One of these profound experiences occurred early in his time with the boys' choir. Thomas tells the story of a cherished toy that played music in his crib. Angela describes it as a merry-go-round mobile that hung above the bed and soothed him greatly as a baby. Even though it had become tattered and only the musicbox remained, it was a keepsake for years. When the family moved to Australia, they left behind many possessions. This was the last Thomas saw of his beloved toy.

T: I realised I had a very emotional bond one day at the choir, with a toy I had once. It was a little wind up toy and it sang The German Lullaby. *When I heard it, it was my first camp I think, and I was like crying after it. I remembered it, I really did miss it.*

C: What was it about that piece of music on it?

T: It was so magical I guess you could say. As soon as we sang that song everything opened up to me. It opened up everything to my childhood.

C: So from that point what changed in you then?

T: I got more clearly into the things I did. I just remember my art teacher told me that I had feeling in my art, the way I drew the eyes and the pupils. I guess I got more into the work I did, more myself.

This critical incident in choir represents for Thomas the point at which he connects music with his identity. Not only does he realise the power of music when associated with emotional memories, he experiences this as a sharpened view of who he is. It is this view that he attributes to the intensity of feeling he experiences in other aspects of his life outside of music, particularly his other passion: drawing.

'I'm a boy, I'm tough, I shouldn't do this kind of thing'

Thomas shows that he is acutely aware of anti-singing discourses. He mocks the hegemonic, masculine stereotype, using a gruff voice: 'I'm a boy, I'm tough, I shouldn't do this kind of thing [sing], I should be roaming around punching up people and making fun of people.' However, this does not seem to represent a deterrent for him at all; it certainly has never stopped him from singing, nor is singing something he only does 'under cover' in choir outside of school. Thomas tells the story of his choice to perform 'Silent Night' as a duet with his younger brother for his Year 6 primary school farewell ceremony. Despite the teasing he anticipated his singing might generate because 'there are a lot of weird people in that school', it was important for him to 'leave an imprint on the school'. Following his performance, he said 'everyone just seemed to respect me, and really share with me the joy of it. The cool kids from the primary school would always say "Man, that's cool", but I wasn't sure if they were mocking me or if they actually meant it so I didn't think about it much. I just took it on board.' He experienced similar recognition in secondary school.

> T: They just respect you with the singing part. Just last time I was in the choir, we were doing music lessons at my school, and I was singing and one of the cool kids in my class asked me to hang out with him at the shopping centre with some 18 year old kids. He is always with other kids; I was a bit surprised by that. I was thinking it was kind of a joke towards me, but he seemed pretty serious about it – he called me a cool kid.
>
> C: Are you going to hang out with him?
>
> T: No. I don't have time for that; I just don't have time for it.

Despite opportunities to be one of the guys, Thomas does not demonstrate any aspiration to associate with the cool kids; he is happy to be making more friends at school with the 'smarter' kids. Thomas is not involved in competitive sports. Angela says that he prefers to read a book, but plays tennis casually and has volunteered for hockey at school. Becoming a chorister has necessitated important choices; the consequences of his decisions have included some friends slipping away, and giving up a lot of leisure time.

> When my friend tried to join [the boys' choir] he got in, but he never joined, he didn't want to. I mean it started making me think again that we were just weird people. I asked why he didn't want to join, he said 'I just don't want to.' He said he wouldn't fit in or something like that. I think people outside are scared of the fact that we can do different stuff to them, that we're superior in the ways that they're weak. I felt a kind of weakness in his voice when he says I don't think I could fit in, or you know – it wouldn't be my type. So I think we have mutual feelings towards each other. And since I was one of them and have become one of these guys now, I can sense that.

What enables Thomas to resist the desire to be 'one of them' despite the costs? Inquiring along these lines may help us find ways to facilitate young people challenging the 'I shouldn't do this kind of thing' pressures. Thomas is aware that choosing to sing is positioning himself on a symbolic level as the 'other'. Presumably he gets relief from singing as a means of coping with his 'otherness'. The irony, from my perspective, is he chooses to cope by doing the thing that positions him as the other/outsider in the first place. However, his otherness is not so straightforward. Thomas inverts the discourse that singing is feminine (weak) by constructing the rejection of singing as an act of weakness, thus singing as an act of superiority (masculinity) signifies its symbolic capital (Bourdieu, 1986). Another aspect of the choir's value, in Thomas's view, is its power as an agent for change, arguably increased by its distinctiveness as something that few males do:

> You can make a good impression, a big impression on a lot of people if you come as a group singing, you know, there's something different out there you can try and you can do.

Opportunities to be unique

What has facilitated opportunities for Thomas to be different and to be accepted? Both Thomas and Angela comment about how supportive his teachers have been. Thomas's music teacher at school, Gary, is a convincing, dynamic person. I visited Thomas's school, a Catholic, single-sex secondary school, on a Friday. I was there to observe a double period of music after lunch, and Gary had my full sympathy! I did not find a class of begrudged youths; Gary had the students 'buzzing' right to when the bell rang. But what struck me was the boys' motivation to participate. Thomas's level of musicianship far exceeds his classmates, which they capitalise on by badgering him for assistance. At one point there was a queue waiting for Thomas's help with a task he finished quickly. Apparently, Thomas's tutoring is a regular occurrence. I thought how fortunate for Gary to have a second teacher in the room, and how fortunate for Thomas to have a place at school where he 'leads the field'. Thomas was part of an environment in which being good at music and singing was made challenging and validated the skills he had gained in choir.

I see Gary as a fast-talking, energetic teacher who after 15 years of teaching at this school went back to the drawing board on a quest to improve his student outcomes. As a result, he became qualified in the Kodály approach and instituted a new curriculum that incorporated singing and solfege; this focus was new for the school, which has a strong band tradition. While it was challenging to get the boys singing in the beginning, Gary was convinced that this would benefit their learning, and he could see the improvements in their musicianship quickly. He also began a Year 7–12, non-auditioned choir the same year, which was in addition to the liturgical choir that performs during services. Being a trumpeter and band leader with little choral experience, taking the choir was challenging for Gary, but was something he was highly committed to.

> I like to develop because I don't want to ever become stale. I've got to be developing and changing and growing and learning. That love of learning is sort of reflected in the students. They go 'oh yeah, he cares, he's really cool. Let's just do it'. It's amazing what you get out of boys … I actually find singing … you don't have to find an instrument. Everyone's got the instrument, it's successful, it's there and they can practise with it at home … So that's really helpful and also it stays with them because they walk out of class singing. They can't walk out of the class playing an instrument. It's not the same.

Gary believes that while the method of teaching is important, the essence of his success as an educator is the relationship he develops with his classes. He says that '[i]t helps being male, tall and charismatic', but believes the students respond most to his genuine enthusiasm for his work. What stood out for me was the atmosphere of participation and expectation he creates among a group of diverse boys. I asked Thomas to describe what a good teacher is, and his response matched my observations of Gary:

> T: If he or she can be tough, but is still not, like, strict. Still always cracks a joke now and then to lighten up the crowd, but still gets the work done. Doesn't waste time and teaches us thoroughly, just tries to inspire us a lot so we can improve.

> C: What sort of inspiration? How do you actually do that?

> T: It depends on the person who's getting inspired, the way they interpret it. Someone could turn into a really good guitar player or something in music. I guess you're trying to achieve something musically. At least something else, if not something musically. Just trying to make them achieve something fun in life that you can always look back to and always do.

Thomas was not motivated to join a choir by some inexplicable drive to sing. He recalls no particular love of singing or ability in his early childhood. Neither of his parents are musicians, although he does describe his family as being very artistic, and refers to an uncle overseas who knows 'practically every instrument'. Angela wrote in the choir newsletter that Thomas 'was always singing around the home, but we might not have thought about a choir if there hadn't been a recruitment visit to his school'. In this sense, Thomas's 'calling' was the opportunity presented to him from the choir's regular recruitment campaign. He needed little more than an invitation to audition for the boys' choir, and has never looked back. But despite being aware of anti-singing discourses, Thomas accepted this invitation when many of his peers, arguably, would have rejected it. He apologises for the idea to accept the invitation not being his own, but in fact being his mother's: 'I'm actually feeling a bit sorry to say this but it was actually my mum who put me into singing'. As we have seen, Angela is also personally invested in the choir as though it is almost a surrogate family and a way of establishing new lives for her boys in a different country. We can recognise how Thomas's values and approach to singing are inflected by Angela's philosophy:

> I've tried to make him understand that you can't be everything and every-body can't be you. You are an individual, so is another person. You're good at something, they're not. So you're not good at something that they are. So you have to learn to adjust.

I asked Thomas a final question: if he could sum up the most important message about his singing. He paused to think, gazing at the floor, then took a deep breath and said: 'We're all unique but we always have the same opportunities to do everything even if we do it differently'.

Concluding remarks

Choral singing has recently enjoyed a resurgence of public support as an art form of great cultural and social value for males and females from diverse walks of life.[3] This emerging picture of choral singing as a powerful and vital part of Australian males' lives counters the popular view that singing is symbolically feminine and thus undesirable for men and boys attempting to achieve the masculine ideal, whatever that may be. Thomas's story is one illustration of a boy who does not aspire to 'just be another kid'. The significance of his story is that his rejection of normative understandings of being a boy is made possible through his singing. Thomas's way of making a mark on his world is by singing. It informs his self-perception as being different from others, and he uses this understanding to position himself as unique. He makes being 'different' an investment by re-articulating choral singing as a powerful act of distinction and, in doing this, he challenges the discourse that this kind of singing is feminine. Thomas is proud of his musical skills, which he promotes to gain respect among his peers, but not without trepidation. Answering what has enabled him to sing despite the fear of social barriers is not simple. His story illustrates that this ability to mobilise singing as a valuable resource is the product of his individual musical pathway, which is the combination of experiences with his mother, teachers, school, peers, the boys' choir and music.

While the uncertainties and inconsistencies in Thomas's story highlight the difficulty in constructing and maintaining a coherent self, he does show unambiguously that singing can be a highly meaningful, multi-layered experience for young boys. He has a deep-felt connection with singing and his interior world; it gives him a great sense of emotional wellbeing and relief from the happenings in his everyday life. Collecting more boys' narratives of singing in various musical contexts may help us reflect on the experiences of boys in our own lives and unveil the multiple ways of being masculine and musical. Spaces, such as the boys' choir, that complicate the notion that singing is feminine, offer fertile ground for further examination of what the boy's voice can represent and the circumstances that may permit more boys to love and continue singing.

Endnotes

1   All names are pseudonyms to protect anonymity.
2   See, for example, the Working Class Men boys choir of Maitland Grossman High School, ABC Radio National link, 'The high school choir for boys': http://www.abc.net.au/rn/lifematters/stories/2007/2012810.htm (accessed 22/01/2009).
3   For example, see the Choir of Hard Knocks, http://www.choirofhardknocks.com.au (accessed 22/01/2009); Music Council of Australia's Life is a Song campaign, http://www.musiccountusin.org.au (accessed on 22/01/2009); Songs in the Key of Bloke community choral festival for males in New South Wales, http://www.mca.org.au/fileadmin/user_upload/mpfl_pdfs/Songs_in_the_Key_of_Bloke.pdf (accessed 22/01/2009).

References

Adler, A. (1999). A Survey of Teacher Practices in Working with Male Singers Before and During the Voice Change, *Canadian Journal of Research in Music Education*, 40(4), pp. 29–33.

Adler, A. (2002). A Case Study of Boys' Experiences of Singing in School, unpublished PhD thesis, Toronto, Canada: University of Toronto.

Adler, A. & Harrison, S.D. (2004). Swinging Back the Gender Pendulum: Addressing boys' needs in music education research and practice, in L. Bartel (ed.), *Research to Practice: Questioning the music education paradigm*, 2, pp. 270–89, Toronto: International Society for Music Education.

Ashley, M. (2006). You Sing Like a Girl? An exploration of 'boyness' through the treble voice, *Sex Education,* 6(2), pp. 193–205.

Austern, L. (1994). 'No Women are Indeed': The boy actor as vocal seductress in late sixteenth- and early seventeenth-century English drama, in L. Dunn & N. Jones (eds), *Embodied Voices: Representing female vocality in Western culture,* pp. 83–102, Cambridge: Cambridge University Press.

Australian Bureau of Statistics (2000, 2003, 2006). *Children's Participation in Cultural and Leisure Activities,* Canberra: Australian Bureau of Statistics.

Bartle, G. (1968). *Music in Australian Schools,* Hawthorn, Victoria: Australian Council for Educational Research.

Bennetts, K. (2008). Boys in Music: A comparative case study of middle school boys' attitudes to music, unpublished PhD thesis. Monash University, Melbourne.

Blaise, M. (2005). *Playing It Straight: Uncovering the gender discourses in the early childhood classroom,* New York: Routledge.

Borgerding, T. (2006). Imagining the Sacred Body: Choirboys, their voices, and Corpus Christi in early modern Seville, in S. Boynton & R. Kok (eds), *Musical Childhoods and the Cultures of Youth,* pp. 25–48, Middletown, CT: Wesleyan University Press.

Bourdieu, P. (1986). The Forms of Capital, in L. Richardson (ed.), *Handbook of Theory and Research for the Sociology of Education,* pp. 241–58, New York: Greenwood Press.

Connolly, P. (2004). *Boys and Schooling in the Early Years,* London: RoutledgeFalmer.

Cooksey, J. (1999). *Working with Adolescent Voices,* St Louis, MO: Concordia Publishing House.

Dame, J. (1994). Unveiled Voices: Sexual difference and the castrato, in P. Brett, E. Wood & G. Thomas (eds), *Queering the Pitch: The new gay and lesbian musicology,* pp. 139–53, New York: Routledge.

Dunn, L. & Jones, N. (eds) (1994). *Embodied Voices: Representing female vocality in Western culture,* Cambridge: Cambridge University Press.

Epstein, D., Kehily, M., Mac an Ghaill, M. & Redman, P. (2001). Boys and Girls Come Out to Play: Making masculinities and femininities in school playgrounds, *Men and Masculinities,* 4(2), pp. 158–72.

Gates, J. (1989). A Historical Comparison of Public Singing by American Men and Women, *Journal of Research in Music Education, 37*(1), pp. 32–47.

Goetze, M., Cooper, N. & Brown, C. (1990). Recent Research on Singing in the General Music Classroom, *Bulletin of the Council for Research in Music Education, 104*, pp. 16–37.

Green, L. (1993). Music, Gender and Education: A report on some exploratory research, *British Journal of Music Education, 10*, pp. 219–53.

Green, L. (1997). *Music, Gender, Education*. Cambridge: Cambridge University Press.

Hall, C. (2003). Understanding and Improving Boys' Singing in the First Year of School, unpublished masters thesis, Monash University, Melbourne.

Hall, C. (2005). Gender and Boys' Singing in Early Childhood, *British Journal of Music Education, 22*(1), pp. 5–20.

Hall, C. (2007). Singing Spaces: Boys getting vocal about singing in and out of school, *Redress, Association of Women Educators, 15*(3), pp. 23–27.

Hall, C. (forthcoming). Voices of Distinction: Choirboys' narratives of music and masculinity, PhD thesis to be submitted to Monash University, Melbourne.

Harrison, S. (2003a). Musical Participation by Boys: The role of gender in the choice of musical activities by males in Australian schools, unpublished PhD thesis, Griffith University, Brisbane.

Harrison, S. (2003b). Music Versus Sport: What's the score? *Australian Journal for Music Education, 1*, pp. 10–15.

Koza, J. (1993). The 'Missing Males' and Other Gender Issues in Music Education: Evidence from the Music Supervisors' Journal, 1914–1924, *Journal of Research in Music Education, 41*(3), pp. 212–32.

Koza, J. (1994). Big Boys Don't Cry (or Sing): Gender, misogyny, and homophobia in college choral methods texts, *The Quarterly Journal of Music Teaching and Learning, 4*(4)/5(1), pp. 48–64.

McClary, S. (1991). *Feminine Endings: Music, gender and sexuality*, Minneapolis: University of Minnesota Press.

O'Toole, P. (1998). A Missing Chapter from Choral Methods Books: How choirs neglect girls, *Choral Journal, 39*(5), pp. 9–32.

Phillips, K. (2003). Creating a Safe Environment for Singing, *Choral Journal, 43*(10), pp. 41–3.

Reay, D. (2002). Shaun's Story: Troubling discourses of white working-class masculinities, *Gender and Education, 14*(3), pp. 221–34.

Shapiro, M. (1994). *Gender and Play on the Shakespearean Stage: Boy heroines and female pages*, Ann Arbor: The University of Michigan Press.

Skelton, C. (2001). *Schooling the Boys: Masculinities and primary education*, Buckingham: Open University Press.

Smith, B. (2001). 'Boys' Business' and Music Education in Top End Schools, Proceedings of the Association of Australian Research in Music Education XXII Annual Conference, Newcastle.

Swain, J. (2004). The Resources and Strategies that 10–11-year-old Boys Use to Construct Masculinities in the School Setting, *British Educational Research Journal*, 30(1), pp. 167–85.

Welch, G. & Howard, D. (2002). Gendered Voice in the Cathedral Choir, *Psychology of Music*, 30, pp. 102–20.

Welch, G., Sergeant, D. & White, P. (1997). Age, Sex and Vocal Task as Factors in Singing In-tune During the First Years of Schooling, *Bulletin of the Council for Research in Music Education, 133*, pp. 153–60.

3 | A boy's music ecosystem

ANITA COLLINS, University of Canberra, Australian Capital Territory

Music teachers around Australia have bemoaned the exodus of boys from school music programs in their early teens. When they seek to understand why this trend occurs, little theoretical or practical research exists, nor does research exist on the wider topic of the specific needs of boys in music education. The greatest wisdom resides with the successful music educators who have consistently maintained participation and engagement levels of boys in their music programs. By comparing the available research and the successful practices of music educators around Australia, a model that exemplified the necessary core beliefs and teaching practices for a successful music education for boys emerged. The model details the delicate and interconnected 'ecosystem' that boys require in order to maintain engagement in their musical activities.

Why does a boy choose to give up clarinet at the age of 13 and take up electric guitar? Why do boys taunt one of their friends because he listens to Mozart while doing his mathematics homework? Why does the boy who loved singing in the choir in primary school suddenly hate all music, other than the newest heavy metal music, and refuse to sing?

As a music educator, I ask myself these questions, and hear them articulated, time and time again by both teachers and parents. From the moment I began to teach in an all-boys environment, this issue perplexed me, and I quickly discovered that I was not alone. Both staff and confused parents consistently raised this issue, and my instincts were confirmed that it was not merely a localised phenomenon when this very issue was raised by fellow educators all around Australia. I felt woefully ill-equipped when advising parents on how to approach this issue effectively, and turned to current research to inform my debate with colleagues on the best methods to alter these trends.

To my astonishment, the answers were not immediately forthcoming from current research. I discovered a body of research that spanned

33

such topics as the heightened creativity of boys in music, the trends in instrumental choice by boys and the late physical development of fine motor skills of boys in relation to musical development. Every one of these areas of research compared the performance of boys to that of girls; very little research focused solely on boys. Much of this research did not originate in Australia, and while giving credence to the fact that this issue has international significance, did not necessarily provide me with solutions that were specific to the Australian educational culture. I found myself piecing together fragments of research from a multitude of sources in order to illuminate my guiding question: how do we as music educators effectively maintain a boy's motivation and engagement in music education in their early secondary school years?

A research snapshot

Finding specific research on this question is difficult from the outset because it bridges two very different areas: music education and gender education. The task of linking the pearls of wisdom from these different areas was a challenge, to say the least, let alone distilling the 'big themes' that emerged. It became clear from the readings that the initial question was not only being asked by my colleagues but also by music educators around the Western world. Many researchers and educators proposed causes for this lack of motivation and engagement: persuasive influence of peer pressures, poor boy-friendly curriculum and teaching strategies, cultural pressures and parental influences just to name a few. Yet, no one had looked at this body of knowledge as a whole, and with just pieces of the puzzle in front of me, I could not yet see the whole picture, and consequently I could not answer my question.

Slowly, the research started to fall into three separate fields: cognitive and emotional development, physical development and social influences. I viewed this research through my music educator glasses and asked myself the question: 'What do I need to know as a music educator from this research?'

What follows are the 'big themes' that emerged during this process.

Cognitive and emotional development

Boys are not great talkers but they learn a lot from 'doing'. As much of the research compared boys with girls, many researchers and educators reported that boys' verbal skills developed later than girls', but their spatial skills developed earlier. This may be a truism of boys' education in general, but if teaching strategies in the music classroom focus more on the absorption and less on the discovery and construction of musical skills and knowledge, then boys are likely to lack engagement. As we all know, managing a practical music lesson is far more challenging on all levels than a 'chalk-and-talk' lesson, but if we wish to maintain the engagement of the boys in our classrooms, we need to re-examine our teaching practices with this research in mind.

Boys need a 'reason' to learn. Boys tend not to cope well with long explanations; they need short, manageable, well-scaffolded and challenging tasks. If a boy is unable to practically apply his new knowledge almost immediately, he sees no reason to retain it. This also has a rippling effect, in that a boy will quickly develop an attitude that musical activities and learning are a waste of time.

Boys like to 'create' music. Just as many boys tend to like to take something apart to see how it works and then put it back together again, many boys like to create musical ideas and put together pieces of music. Composition was found to be both a highly engaging activity for boys as well as an area in which boys excelled above girls in levels of complexity and musicality.

Boys respond to a high level of teacher involvement and interaction. It was found that boys displayed a higher level of confidence, persistence, engagement and independence when their teachers maintained a high level of interaction with them. Just as boys need small and manageable tasks to maintain their engagement, they respond positively to the consistent involvement of their teachers in their efforts. Many music educators would attest to the need to 'keep a watchful eye' on the boys in their classroom, but the research shows that if turned to a positive interaction rather than a negative one, boys' engagement levels in the subject increases.

Music is not a 'manly' thing to do. This comment is all too common, and in a cognitive and emotional sense, it leads to a negative attitude towards all musical activities. This attitude, then, has an incredibly strong influence on boys' engagement in music in general. At 13 and 14 years of age, the opinions of a boy's peers, and even his parents, are extremely influential; as such, a statement like this can completely shut down his interest in musical activities.

Music education needs to start early in life. This is a widely accepted principle, but for boys it has a significant influence as they enter their secondary school years. Boys who reach a moderate level of proficiency on their musical instrument by the time they enter secondary school are more likely to continue playing their instrument into their later secondary school years than those boys who either begin learning an instrument quite late in their primary years or at the beginning of secondary school.

This has implications for music activities being coordinated as K–12 programs, not segregated into primary and secondary.

Physical development

Boys' fine motor skills develop later than girls. We have all seen how a 14-year-old boy can grow 10 centimetres during the summer holidays and then proceed to bump into every desk and door they come across, and show a marked lack of coordination for the following 6 months. This alone can be a difficult period for any boy, but when we factor in the learning of a musical instrument and pressure for peer acceptance, it becomes far worse. Guiding and supporting a boy through this period requires empathy, humour and persistence from music educators.

Boys and singing; a perennial mystery. This issue raised the most passionate disagreement and argument from both researchers and music educators. Some said boys love to sing, but are concerned about quality. Some said boys in general were all tone deaf. Some said boys don't like to sing. All agreed that involving boys in singing is a delicate balancing act and depends significantly on the school culture, choice of repertoire, performance opportunities and teaching strategies.

Music activities are stressful for boys. Although girls reported that they felt anxious and stressed during musical performance, when physiological responses were monitored during a performance it was actually the boys who experienced higher heart and blood pressure rates. For boys, the choice to engage in a musical performance is more likely to lead to real physiological effects, and could very well lead to boys disengaging in musical activities for a very physical reason. For music educators, this means a different approach to performance preparation, and the type of performance boys are engaged in.

Social influences

There are 'boy' instruments and 'girl' instruments. Numerous studies have been done on instrument choice and gender, and the correlation among these is alarming. Stereotyping of instruments is influenced by the media, parents and peers, but interestingly does not begin until nine years of age. This information can be incredibly useful for music educators when designing instrumental programs. In general, higher string instruments (violin and viola) and higher woodwind instruments (flute, oboe and clarinet) are 'girl' instruments. In an all-boys school this has implications for starting and maintaining a string or symphony orchestra, as well as an evenly balanced concert band. Just like boys and singing, this area of music education is strongly affected by a critical mass of students playing 'girlie' instruments. It is difficult to determine what a critical mass might be; an example could be 25 boys playing flute in a music program of 180 boys. When this critical mass occurs, the activity turns from being an unacceptable pursuit for a young man to an acceptable and 'normal' activity. Music educators need to positively discriminate towards instrument groups that are perceived to be 'girlie' in order to counter the extremely pervasive influence of their peers, parents and, particularly, fathers.

Music is a girl's subject. There were some wonderful quotes in the research about how *music is not a real job* and *music is not something that real men do*. The topic of what a *real* man might be is a discussion for another time, but this pervading belief comes from parents, peers and non-music educators. Music educators and researchers alike highlighted this belief as one that needed to be constantly monitored and overtly challenged. Many commented that success and high-quality performances made the best antidote.

Parents need to support boys in their musical activities. It was identified that boys whose parents openly supported them in their musical activities had high levels of motivation and engagement. This seems so simple, but just as the higher levels of interaction of teachers affect boys' engagement, so does the attendance of parents at concerts. Showing an explicit interest in their son's musical progress and supporting him by dropping him off at workshops and taking him to musical performances are all vital. As music educators, we would all love to have a group of parents just like this, but if a parent has not experienced the benefits and joys of a positive music education for themselves, they may not know how to support their sons. Working with parents to give them opportunities to grow themselves as musicians and music lovers is an important focus for music educators.

Being involved in musical activities can call 'masculinity' into question. In a nutshell, boys at age 14 generally don't want anything they do to lead to an accusation that they are anything other than a heterosexual male. If we put together all the preconceptions that music is a girl's subject, certain instruments should be played by girls and girls are better at music than boys, then it is no wonder this assumption is made. This doesn't stop boys playing music, but to reinforce their masculinity they tend to choose certain socially acceptable forms of music making. It is the boy who has played violin for five years, and seemingly loved the instrument, but suddenly announces he is going to give it up at the age of 14 to play bass guitar. For many boys, this influence is very strong and almost an imperative. As music educators we know the signs, and managing this period for boys and for our music programs can be frustrating and bewildering.

A boy's music ecosystem

It is clear that what motivates and engages boys in music education, both before and during their early secondary school years, stems from factors both inside and outside the classroom. The messages and experiences influence their thoughts and choices, and these are all contained in the complex cultural ecosystem that surrounds each boy in his early secondary school years. For the purposes of my metaphor, an ecosystem is a system in which members benefit from each other's participation. The boy is the centre of the ecosystem, and surrounding him is a web of messages and experiences about music and musical activities, created by the people with whom he interacts. If the interactions are positive and 'healthy' for the boy, the ecosystem and the boy thrive, if they are negative and 'harmful' for the boy, the ecosystem becomes contaminated and rapidly dies, along with the boy's motivation and engagement in music education.

To give you an understanding of a boy's music ecosystem, let me begin with a synthesis of the research. By combining qualitative and quantitative research techniques with a mixed-methods approach, three central themes, or essences, emerged.

Essences of a boy's music ecosystem

An *essence* is the most crucial part, the indispensable or intrinsic property, or the most important ingredient. Let's begin with a simple list of common themes throughout the research literature.

What motivates and engages boys in music education?

- Challenge, risk, engagement, interest and positive attitude
- Success and praise from male role models
- Accomplishment which is quick and noticeable
- Positive parental support, which supports music as being an expression of masculinity and a good means of forming a boy's identity
- Technology, because it enables boys to create compositions quickly.

What discourages and disengages boys in music education?

- Public misunderstanding, both of the nature of learning music and questions concerning a boy's masculinity and sexuality
- Non-acceptance by peers

- Negative influences by role models, such as parents, coaches, siblings, teachers
- Physical development, which hampers musical development such as voice changes and later development of fine motor skills than girls
- Conflict between sporting interests and musical interests, where sport will almost invariably win.

These two lists are mirror images of each other, and thus the concept of an interconnected and interdependent ecosystem was the most appropriate vehicle to illustrate the relationship. So what motivates and engages boys in music? For a boy to continue his musical activities during his secondary school years, the healthy ecosystem that surrounds him must contain three key factors, each containing two complementary aspects:

1   A genuine *interest* in music and a *positive attitude* towards the subject
2   A sensation of *success* and measurable *accomplishment*; for example, on his chosen instrument
3   A sense of *acceptance* by his peers as well as genuine *praise* for his musical activities, especially from male role models.

If the ecosystem becomes contaminated, as is discussed later, these contrary factors emerge and act as a negative influence on a boy's motivation and engagement in music.

1   A *lack of interest* in the subject, possibly due to teaching methods that have not actively engaged and motivated the creative and practical sides of a boy's character. This then leads to a *negative attitude* towards the subject in general.
2   A perceived *lack of success*, which is especially damaging when a boy compares himself to his peers, particularly girls. Boys quickly 'weigh up' the prospect of success in any pursuit, and if they perceive a *lack of accomplishment*, then it draws the inevitable question from a boy's perspective: 'Why should I put my energy into this activity?'
3   The *reinforcement of negative stereotypes* about masculinity. The perception that 'music is for girls' automatically leads to the understanding that it is not an appropriate pursuit for a man. Similarly, if a boy does continue to pursue music in his adolescent years, his sexuality can be called into question.

Understanding these three essences is important, but it is how these essences interact that is crucial. For a boy to maintain his interest in music, he must have an ecosystem that contains all three motivating factors:

- Essence 1 – interest and positive attitude
- Essence 2 – success and accomplishment
- Essence 3 – acceptance and praise.

As mentioned earlier, positive interactions enrich the ecosystem, while negative interactions pollute it. Let me share a story of how a boy's music ecosystem can alter from a healthy state to a contaminated state through a few ill-placed messages and experiences.

ABOUT A BOY

The situation
A boy does not achieve success quickly when he begins to learn his instrument. This could be due to a lack of consistent practice or unsuitability of the instrument to his physique.

The contamination
The cycle begins with a boy questioning why he is not achieving. He begins to feel insecure about his skills and compares himself to those who are experiencing success.

As the boy experiences little success on his instrument, his level of interest wanes and his previously positive attitude begins to become negative, not only towards his instrument but towards musical pursuits in general. The effort required to continue practising without a measurable level of accomplishment becomes even harder to muster when he sees himself compared to classmates, especially girls, who are excelling on their instruments.

Finally, the messages the boy has heard from his parents, peers and the media about masculinity and music come into play. It is a common human trait to want to be successful at any activity we do, so not experiencing success is not something we like to show to others. In this case, the boy might feel that he needs to find another reason for giving up his instrument, a reason other than that he was unable to be successful at it. This is where such comments as 'none of my friends are playing instruments' or 'music is for girls' may be used.

Figure 3.1: About a boy

In my experience, boys often swap to a different instrument or join a different ensemble before giving up music entirely. I have experienced a trend in which boys, after struggling to understand peer pressure and their changing bodies have, at around the age of 16 or 17 years, realised the importance of music in their lives. Consequently, they have rekindled their musical studies and have gained greater confidence in their own individual characters and decision-making skills, but these instances are atypical of the general trend.

As a teacher, knowledge of these factors when teaching boys, writing curriculum and encouraging a positive school culture are vital. By using this knowledge it may be possible to identify strategies that teachers can use to combat such contamination of a boy's music ecosystem. If teachers are able to gain a clear understanding of what both motivates and discourages boys, they will be better equipped to deal with the boy who shows a profound lack of interest in the subject, or one who suddenly wants to quit music after several years of participation. It appears that the closer a teacher may be able to get to the 'real reason' behind a boy's frame of mind concerning music, the greater effect they will be able to have on the situation or trend.

To test the validity of my essences, I conducted a series of interviews from three focus groups (directors of music, classroom music educators and Year 11 music students) from three schools around Australia. The schools were chosen for their similar structure: all were single-sex boys private schools, all had maintained high levels of participation of a large proportion of the school population in musical activities into their senior secondary school years and all had maintained this participation level and high standards of achievement in state examinations for longer than 10 years consecutively.

A boy's music habitat

To continue with the metaphor, seven elements contribute to a boy's motivation and engagement in music in his early secondary school years. These surround the boy and all impact of the central essences of a boy's music ecosystem. The seven elements are:

- Element 1 – school culture
- Element 2 – relationships
- Element 3 – peers
- Element 4 – parents
- Element 5 – role models
- Element 6 – student character
- Element 7 – teaching strategies.

It is within each of these elements that the relative 'health' of the boy's music ecosystem is defined. The messages boys receive and the experiences they gain in these seven elements is pivotal to their effective and consistent involvement in music education. What follows are my recommendations on the significant policies, organisational structures and teaching strategies that can affect boys' motivation and engagement in music education.

School culture

✓ School expectation to be involved in musical activities
✓ Promoting understanding of music as an art form
✓ Music at school functions
✓ Support from the leadership team of the school
✓ Recognition of musicians by the school community
✓ Allowing boys to be both sportsmen and musicians
✓ Many levels of achievement built into the program
✓ Whole-school music experiences
✓ Acceptance and respect of musicians

Teaching strategies

✓ Consistency of staff
✓ Understanding boys' individual motivation
✓ Exposure to high-quality performances
✓ Start music education early (Years 4–9)
✓ Constant positive reinforcement
✓ Lessons that involve 65% practical activities and 35% theoretical activities
✓ Fast-paced lessons
✓ Challenging curriculum

Relationships

✓ Meaningful interactions with peers and staff
✓ Open display of a passion for music
✓ Staff understanding a boy's motivation for his involvement in music
✓ Staff who have strong interpersonal skills
✓ Staff who can relate to boys
✓ Genuine interest in each boy as an individual

Student character

✓ Confident, independent and individualistic characters
✓ The fulfilment and avenues for expression a boy finds in music must withstand peer pressure, parental disinterest and other obstacles

Peers

✓ Boys who have musicians as friends and who are of a similar age and musical ability
✓ Boys who have friends who are musically educated and accepting

Success and accomplishment

Praise and acceptance

Interest and positive attitude

Parents

✓ Parents who are supportive of their sons' interest in music
✓ Parents who attend concerts
✓ Parents who encourage their sons to learn a music instrument at a young age
✓ Parents who express their acceptance of music as a pursuit for boys

Role models

✓ Role models who are real and genuine people
✓ Role models who are trusted by boys to tell them when they get it right and wrong
✓ Role models who give genuine and consistent praise
✓ Role models who can relate on a musical and a personal level

Figure 3.2: A healthy music ecosystem for boys

School culture

The most influential factor for the success of any music program is a school culture that openly and positively supports music. Similarly, an unequivocal expectation that all students who attend a school will be involved in some form of musical activity is a powerful motivator. The school leadership must openly and frequently support musical activities and recognise musical achievement on the same level as sporting achievement. Similarly, the timetable structures of a school must allow for every boy to be a sportsman *and* a musician. Boys should not have to choose between the two pursuits.

High-quality music education is vital to engendering a culture of musical participation. Students should come to understand the fundamentals of music so that they may understand and artistically appreciate all music. In order to acknowledge success, variety performance, composition and live music opportunities must be built into the music program. All students have to experience music as an art form, and the musical experiences must promote a deep understanding of music as well as an acceptance of, and respect for, musicians. Schools should include some type of whole–school musical experience, where the students are the actual musicians, such as a whole–school choral item, communal singing at the beginning of each assembly and whole year-group musical performances for parents. Music, performed by school musicians, must be a fixture at school functions, particularly events such as sporting presentations and parent evenings.

Relationships

To succeed, boys, far more than girls, rely on positive relationships in their educational environment. These positive relationships revolve around a boy believing that a staff member is genuinely interested in him. Boys respond to staff who have strong interpersonal skills and can easily relate to them. There must be meaningful interactions between both the boy and the music staff, and his musical and non-musical peers. Music, being an expressive art form, attracts boys to it for very personal reasons, and boys respond positively to staff who show an understanding of their attraction. Finally, boys need to be able to share their passion for music in a safe environment, where there is mutual trust, respect and acceptance.

Peers

Every focus group identified that if the number of boys actively involved in music is over 50 per cent of the school population, then a greater number of boys will continue to be involved in musical activities until the end of Year 12. There is a level of critical mass required to create a positive music culture within a school. Boys, especially around the age of 13–15 years old, are highly influenced by their peers. Of all the music students I spoke to, the single most influential factor that kept them involved in music was either having musicians as friends who were of a similar age and musical ability, or having friends who were musically educated and accepting; a positive culture through strength in numbers.

Parents

During their secondary schools years, boys rely more readily on the opinions of their peers, rather than the opinions of their parents. However, parents have a significant role to play in a boy's belief that music is an acceptable and positive pursuit. Both music educators and music students identify that parental support and acceptance of their interest in music is a vital factor. Similarly, the parents' act of attending a concert to see their son perform means a great deal to a boy. Many music students identified that it was their parents' encouragement that drove them to take up a musical instrument at a young age. However, students who reached a moderate level of competency on their instrument by Year 7 did not experience any thoughts of giving up their instrument. They generally felt little pressure from their peers to discontinue their musical activities, and reported a sense of continued development and success. Even those students who changed instruments for any reason found a way to duplicate their sense of success and utilise their previous musical training, and therefore continued their involvement in musical activities. It appears that starting boys on an instrument between the ages of 4 and 9 years and receiving instrumental lessons before commencing secondary school is imperative for continued motivation and engagement.

Role models

There has been a focus on the importance of role models in boys' education generally in recent years, particularly on significant male role models for boys. In keeping with this focus, an emphasis on explicit positive and negative models of male sexuality and masculinity in terms of music education were expected. Interestingly, music students had little preference for a given stereotype; they respected role models who were men and women, who were real and genuine people and who gave them genuine and consistent praise. For boys, authenticity and sincerity emerged as the deciding factors. The boys found role models who were honest and willing to tell them when they had 'got it right, and got it wrong' the most appealing. Most significantly, and particular to the field of music, students responded to those role models with whom they could relate on an equal musical footing and enjoy sharing their passion for music.

Student character

Music is only one of many art forms, and is most definitely not the only form of human expression. Consequently, not all boys take up music as an interest outside the classroom. However, there are certain characteristics that emerged in student musicians that were easily identifiable by both music educators and music students. Student musicians are confident, independent and have individualistic characters.

Through music, boys can also develop a stronger sense of self, sometimes because the challenges help them build up a level of resilience. Many music students identified that they had become more self-assured by the mere fact that other students had bullied them for being musicians. The music student's unwillingness to succumb to peer pressure had actually made them more confident in their individual choices. The fulfilment and avenues for expression that a boy finds in music must withstand peer pressure, parental disinterest and other obstacles, yet each experience can be either character building or character destroying, depending on the individual boy. It is not known if such character traits are present in students who discontinued their music education in their early secondary school.

Teaching strategies

As educators, we all have what we believe to be a toolbox of tried-and-true methods or activities that produce the best results. When comparing the results of what music educators and music students felt were the most successful tools, a surprisingly short list emerges. Within the classroom, the most successful tools are fast-paced lessons that divide into 65 per cent practical activities and 35 per cent theoretical activities (this division was also quoted at 70/30 by a number of educators and students). Educators need to understand each boy's individual motivation for studying music and must give constant genuine and positive reinforcement. Music education must begin between the ages of 4 and 9 years of age, so as to allow for a sufficient level of competency by the time a boy enters secondary school. Students must have exposure to high-quality performances, not just school concerts and fête performances. The curriculum must be challenging and allow for boys to explore their areas of interest as well as be exposed to music and areas of study they would not otherwise experience. Finally, the consistency and stability of music personnel over a number of years is an important factor for boys, as the trust and time that boys invest in the relationships they have with the staff can only occur over a number of years. This has implications for school leadership on their treatment, development and rewarding of their staff.

Conclusion

So, what can a music educator, or a music department, do with this knowledge?

The answer is to *evaluate*. Look at all the areas of your program and identify which ones you do very well, and which ones have not been successful. Brainstorm ways of altering the status quo, and think outside the square when you do this: you might be surprised by what you find. Ask your peers and do some research; you can guarantee that other music educators are having the same frustrations and successes as you are; learn from them. Tailor modifications to your school; every school's culture and expectations are different and will require a unique approach. You know your school culture well; use that knowledge. Involve your school leadership; cultural change involves everyone and is most powerful coming from the top. Don't be afraid to put forward ways you would like your school leadership team to assist you; if you all mould the message there is a greater likelihood of success. And then evaluate again. You are largely in control of the ecosystem that surrounds your young musicians, and it is a system that needs persistent and appropriate attention. This process is long, it is fulfilling and it requires commitment and constant refinement.

Much like learning music.

Bibliography

Abel, J.L. & Larkin, K.T. (1990). Anticipation of Performance Among Musicians: Physiological arousal, confidence, and state-anxiety, *Psychology of Music, 18*(2), pp. 171–82.

Abeles, H. & Porter, S. (1978). Sex-Stereotyping of Musical Instruments, *Journal of Research in Music Education, 26*(2) (Summer), pp. 65–75.

Asmus, E.P. Jr (1986). Student Beliefs About the Causes of Success and Failure in Music: A study of achievement motivation, *Journal of Research in Music Education, 26*(4), pp. 262–78.

Collins, A. (2005). Boys and Music: What encourages boys to remain involved and motivated in Music Education in their secondary school years?, unpublished masters thesis, Deakin University, Victoria.

Green, L. (1993). Music, Gender and Education, A Report on Some Exploratory Research, *British Journal of Music Education*, 10(3), pp. 219–54.

Keddie, A. (2005). A Framework for 'Best Practice' in Boys' Education: Key requisite knowledges and productive pedagogies, *Pedagogy, Culture and Society*, 13(1), pp. 59–74.

Koza, J.E. (1993). Missing Males and Other Gender Issues in Music Education: Evidence from the Music Supervisors' Journal, 1914–1924', *The Journal of Research in Music Education*, 41(3), pp. 212–32.

Levitin, D.J. (2006) *This Is Your Brain on Music: The science of a human obsession*, New York: Dutton/Penguin.

Mills, M., Martino, W. & Lingard B. (2007). Getting Boys' Education 'Right': The Australian Government's Parliamentary Inquiry Report as an exemplary instance of recuperative masculinity politics, *British Journal of Sociology of Education*, 28(1), pp. 5–21.

Sadker, M.P. & Sadker, D.M. (1988). Sexism in Education, in B.A. Stitt et al. (eds), *Building Gender Fairness in Schools*, pp. 19–57, Carbondale: Southern Illinois University Press.

Trollinger, L.M. (1993/4). Sex/Gender Research in Music Education: A review, *Quarterly Journal of Music Teaching and Learning*, 4(4)–5(1), pp. 22–39.

Weaver-Hightower, M. (2003). The 'Boy Turn' in Research on Gender and Education, *Review of Educational Research*, 73(4), pp. 471–98.

Webster, P.R. (1979). Relationship Between Creative Behaviour in Music and Selected Variables as Measured in High School Students, *Journal of Research in Music Education*, 27(4), pp. 227–42.

West, P. (2001). *Ideas Schools Could Use to Increase Boys' Achievement: Recommendations from the report on best practice in boys' education*, Sydney: Research Group on Men and Families & Men's Health Information and Resource Centre, University of Western Sydney.

Zdzinski, S.F. (1992). Relationships Among Parental Involvement, Music Aptitude, and Musical Achievement of Instrumental Music Students, *Journal of Research in Music Education*, 40 (2), pp. 114–25.

4 Music making in adolescence and beyond

SCOTT D. HARRISON, Griffith University, Queensland

Recent studies have indicated that, while gender stereotypes are entrenched from early childhood, the most significant change in participation takes place in the transition from primary school to secondary school, with the onset of adolescence.

In this chapter, the reasons for this change are heard through two voices: through background information from recent studies and through the voices of men reflecting on their experiences of music at school and the deterrents they encountered. It also refers to possible solutions that might assist in breaking down barriers from home, school and societal perspectives. As such, it presents both academic research and practical ideas for parents, schools and teachers, to assist in addressing the lack of participation by males.

The first part of the chapter is devoted to some of the background information about participation in music, and asks the questions:

Why participate? A rationale and advocacy perspective in relation to the engagement of males in music

Who participates? Some data on participation rates in music and instrument choice

What causes non-participation? A focus on some of the reasons as to why males do not participate in the arts

How can teachers and parents overcome reluctance? Some strategies from recent international and Australian studies to assist in engagement in music

The last part of the chapter takes the stories of two men, Brian and Brett, who reflect on their experiences of school. In so doing, some personal perspectives are added to background information from the first part of the chapter, to assist in managing adverse circumstances and increasing engagement of males in music.

Why participate?

The National Review of School Music Education (Pascoe, Leong, MacCallum, Mackinlay et al., 2005) found that while some students had access to music at school, many more did not participate or participated solely in informal environments. Music teachers, according to Black (2004) may feel as though they are on the margin and their subject is not part of the school's core business; hence, their students, especially the boys, are reluctant learners and their parents 'dubious supporters'. This is further exacerbated, because some benefits from engagement with the arts are not immediately apparent. In *The Evaluation of School-based Arts Education Programmes in Australian Schools* (Bryce, Mendelovits, Beavis, McQueen et al., 2004), the suggestion is made that in addition to having intrinsic value, the arts can be an important medium for developing 'enabling' metacognitive skills and attitudes. In sites evaluated by Bryce et al. (2004), there was a sense that arts programs were providing valuable, positive learning experiences.

Participation in the arts goes beyond traditional classroom spaces and time frames. Co-curricular activities are intrinsic to arts learning in schools, but the value of these experiences has been under-researched. In a study by Marsh and Kleitman (2002), participation in extracurricular school activities was found to benefit students on a number of key criteria, including school grades, homework, educational and occupational aspirations, self-esteem, being free from substance abuse and attaining a higher educational level. Participation in school-based extracurricular activity was shown to have more benefits than participation in out-of-school activities, including quantifiable outcomes in school grades, university enrolment and ultimate educational level. Findings from the research of Eccles, Barber, Stone and Hunt (2003) support the conclusion that extracurricular school activity fosters commitment that subsequently enhances diverse academic outcomes, particularly for socio-economically disadvantaged students who are not catered for by the traditional educational curriculum. Temmerman (2007) cites the school production as the prime site for developing generic skills and attributes, asserting that:

> ... the attributes of innovative thinking and interpretation, problem solving, co-operative decision making and effective communication, so crucial to being a successful citizen in the new economy, are central and natural to arts education. (p. 9)

In *How Popular Musicians Learn*, Lucy Green (2001) claims that popular musicians learn generic life skills through peer-based learning. Pitts' (2005) work with high-school students demonstrated that school students valued music as a potential source of confirmation and confidence, an opportunity to demonstrate or acquire skills and an opportunity to perform with others.

Who participates, who doesn't?

Having established the benefits of interaction with music in a variety of contexts, the question arises as to who participates in musical activities in the adolescent years. Longitudinal studies have provided statistics indicating that enrolments in the arts in school have grown in the recent years. Fullarton, Walker, Ainley and Hillman (2003) noted that from 1993 to 2001, almost one-third of all Year 12 students were enrolled in the arts. Enrolments in the performing arts increased by around 3.4 percentage points from 1998 to 2001 and, specifically in music, by 1.3 percentage points. Overall, there was a small increase in the curriculum share for the arts from 7 per cent to 8 per cent between 1990 and 2001, with an increase in music enrolments from 4 per cent to 6 per cent. In terms of gender, females are more likely than males to be enrolled in arts disciplines, with a ratio of females to males of 2.2:1.0 (Fullarton et al., 2003). Gender, language background and school sector were found to have an independent effect on subject participation in the arts.

In relation to involvement in the arts during non-school hours, the Australian Bureau of Statistics *Survey of Children's Participation in Cultural and Leisure Activities* (2006) provides some revealing data. In a survey of 2,664,700 children aged 5 to 14 years, an estimated 33 per cent (869,600) of children were involved in at least one of four selected cultural activities (playing a musical instrument, singing, dancing and drama) in their non-school hours. In the year to April 2006, 20 per cent of 5 to 14 year olds played a musical instrument outside of school.

The survey indicates that these activities were more popular with girls than boys. Approximately 44 per cent (572,400) of girls and 22 per cent (297,200) of boys were involved in at least one of the selected cultural activities. The following graphs illustrate the nature of engagement in cultural activities by sex (Figure 4.1) and age (Figure 4.2).

Overall, participation rates increased with age, peaking at 39 per cent for those aged 10 years and then dropping to 34 per cent for those aged 14 years. It is the downward trend beginning at age 13 that is of interest in this chapter.

To narrow the focus from broad engagement in the arts, Harrison (2004) researched the instrument preferences of students in secondary schools. In a study spanning three years, 950 students were asked to indicate the instruments they learned. Figure 4.3 gives an indication of the instrument preferences across the three years.

Figure 4.1: Participation in organised cultural activities, by sex

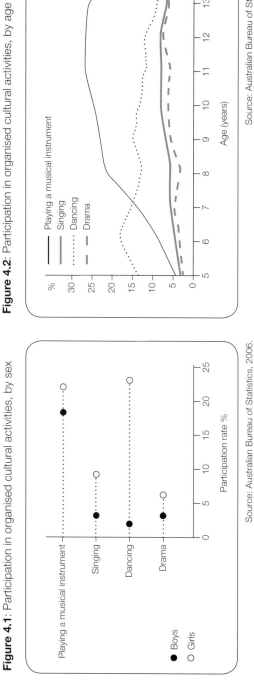

Source: Australian Bureau of Statistics, 2006.

Figure 4.2: Participation in organised cultural activities, by age

Source: Australian Bureau of Statistics, 2006.

Figure 4.3: Comparison of instrument selection by secondary students

	Flt	Ob	Clt	Bsn	Sax	Tpt	Tbn	FH	Tba	Vln	Vla	VC	Db	Hp	Gtr	Voice	Pno	Perc	Comp
Average % of males	9	34	27	38	42	67	97	66	77	22	11	40	65	0	74	10	46	67	11
Average % of females	91	66	73	62	58	33	3	34	23	78	89	60	35	100	26	90	54	33	89

Key: Flt = flute, Ob = oboe, Clt = clarinet, Bsn = bassoon, Sax = saxophone, Tpt = trumpet, Tbn = trombone, FH = French Horn, Tba = Tuba, Vln = Violin, Vla = Viola, VC= violoncello, Db = double bass, Hp = harp, Gtr = guitar, Voice = voice, Pno = piano, Perc = percussion, Comp = composition   Source: Harrison, 2004.

The polarisation of instruments to the stereotypical choice is quite clear when viewed across the three years. Flute, viola, harp, voice and composition are very strongly represented by females. Percussion and lower brass are the domain of males.[1]

Ensemble studies form the basis of many school programs at this age. The sex-stereotyping of instruments described above potentially can affect ensemble balance. Anecdotally, teachers report that while symphony orchestras and concert bands show an even representation of males and females, string ensembles typically had twice the number of girls than boys and up to three-quarters of choirs were girls.

As a result of these studies of instrument preference and ensemble participation, the *Gender Hierarchy of Musical Paradigms* (Adler & Harrison, 2004) was adapted for the Australian environment to account for genre differences (for example, marching bands have been omitted). The resulting hierarchy is represented in Figure 4.4.

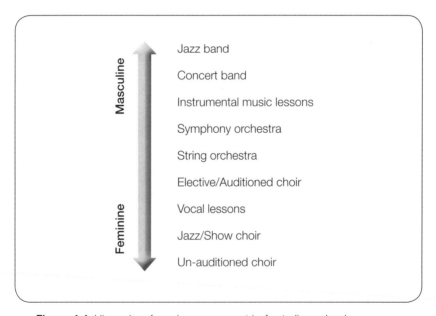

Figure 4.4: Hierarchy of music engagement in Australian schools

Source: Adapted from Adler and Harrison, 2004, p. 279.

A hierarchy of this kind allows for a critical examination of instruments and ensembles and the ways in which they are affected by sex-stereotyping and gender influences. The adolescent years are significantly problematic for balanced engagement, and the factors behind gendered associations are of interest if the trends are to be reversed.

What causes non-participation?

Possible factors affecting school music participation, as identified by Siebenaler (2006), included family, peer pressure, gender roles and the voice change. The effect of gender, as evidenced in Figures 4.3 and 4.4 above, is of particular concern. Both males and females are disadvantaged by the gender order. Green (1993) describes the reality of the classroom and rehearsal environment succinctly:

> ... both boys and girls tended to restrict themselves or find themselves restricted to certain musical activities for fear of intruding into the other sex's territory, where they may have been accused of some sort of musical transvestism. (p. 248)

Rigby (1997) noted that boys reported being bullied more frequently in secondary schools, while Ainley, Collins, Batten and Getty (1996) indicated that over 80 per cent of secondary students and over 90 per cent of primary students reported sex-based name calling (p. 163). While homophobic harassment is prevalent across all age groups, it is particularly evident among boys during the transition from primary school to secondary school. This transitory stage has some implication for musical participation. The word 'poofter' is introduced in the middle years of primary school, but the label can gain sexual meaning in the secondary school, at the transition into Year 7 or 8, when older boys are responsible for inducting younger boys (Plummer, 1999, p. 41). Boys will therefore go to considerable length to distance themselves from any association with femininity, for fear of being labelled a 'poof' (Martino, 1995). Adult males interviewed for this chapter reflected on their experiences of school at this transitory stage, and the price of performing music. Matthew[2] commented:

> Then came high school. It was no longer 'cool' to do music. From the moment I started high school to the year I finished, came the taunting. The name-calling started. Poofter, Faggot, Queer. You name it, I copped it!

Green (1996) and Harrison (2001) noted that to perform certain styles of music could bring credit and reduce the exclusion from socialisation through bullying. This was certainly the case in relation to performing music theatre and pop music. One participant, Gary, noted that while there were homosexual associations with performing music theatre, his passion overcame this and his peers came to accept his desire to perform:

> In Year 11 and 12 with school productions, suddenly music, acting and singing were accepted by the majority of students. I really loved the productions because I had been so lonely.

Similarly, gender-role rigidity in males' engagement with music was also a feature of males' comments. Boys typically did not engage with the instruments at the non-stereotypical end of the spectrum, but when they did, they frequently changed their mind in the adolescent years, as Craig noted:

> When I reached Year 7 for some reason I decided to give it (violin) up and let it all slide, for reasons unknown to me. I stopped practising and stopped lessons … I wanted a normal and enjoyable childhood. I think this came from the pressures my parents put on me as well as teachers, to succeed and be the best.

The effect of role models was a feature in many of the interviews. Students indicated a preparedness to change their gendered viewpoint when confronted with high-quality role models, as Greg stated:

> During my time in high school I developed a great love of music and it soon became my greatest concern in life. Thanks mainly to the music teachers at that time, we were given the opportunity to do and see things that your average student would not … it was during this part of my life that I began thinking about continuing music as a full time career.

How can teachers and parents overcome reluctance?

In addition to role models as positive influence, Siebenaler (2006) comments that while there are many factors to consider (and not all are in the realm of the music educator), 'positive, quality, meaningful music experiences in elementary and middle school would encourage students to continued participation' (p. 8). This volume abounds with examples of positive, quality and meaningful experiences in schools. Other examples in recent literature include Harrison (2004), Hissey (2004) and Paye (2005). As a music educator working in Sydney, Hissey (2004), for example, notes that:

> …. success in retention of boys in music has involved the full support of the College administration … For music to be recognized and valued by a school it has to be seen to contribute to its fuller life; it has to do this well and often and in many different ways—from the encouragement of rock bands, to providing quality liturgical performances of sacred music. (p. 6)

In 2004, Harrison provided a range of strategies for boys' involvement in choirs, including selection of repertoire, flexible scheduling and provision of a variety of opportunities for involvement. Paye (2005) concurs with these suggestions, adding that the opportunity for leadership is important for adolescent boys, along with the setting of clear objectives. Ultimately, strategies are useless without an investment in human resources. Support of school administrators who have a zero tolerance to bullying and a commitment to the employment of role models from the ranks of teachers, peers and community representatives are critical in achieving success in the adolescent years. The quotes above give snapshots of the experiences of males as they reflect on their adolescent years. The narratives below give a more complete picture of the role of music across the life span, and particularly at this critical transition stage.

Stories of men and boys

The experiences expressed here represent the reflections of two males' engagement in music across the lifespan.

About Brian

At the time of writing, Brian was 19 years old. He was born in Brisbane. He had attended Catholic primary and secondary schools. Brian is the eldest in his family and has a younger brother and a younger sister. He is currently completing undergraduate studies in music.

Brian's story

Early recollections and primary school days
Right from the moment I entered the world it seemed I had a special connection with music. My father recalls to me now the many nights I would wake up disturbed in the middle of the night. The only way I would calm down was if Dad took me to the window and sang a song that he had made up about me. From these early experiences it seemed music had a place in my life that satisfied something nothing else would.

When I was nine years of age the classroom music teacher advertised guitar lessons at the school. I begged my parents to let me learn. They did and also bought me a ¾ size guitar. This was the beginning of a love affair that has only grown stronger to the present day. Up until I began learning guitar I had been struggling with a learning disorder and not doing well at school. It was only when I started learning guitar that I really began to read properly. My teachers were amazed at the difference in my schoolwork. My first guitar teacher was a man who really instilled a love of music in me. He encouraged me to write my own songs and gave me many opportunities to perform these.

>>

The transition to high school

High school was very much a formation period for me as a musician, along with all areas of life. It was music at high school that gave me a focus for everything else. Therefore it was very important that, as an extremely enthusiastic and also quite sensitive 13-year-old, the music staff gave the right support. The director of music encouraged me to compose and gave me performance opportunities when he could. He constantly guided me whilst never making me be something I was not.

Coping with adversity

It was the support of people like this at my school that really helped me survive at high school. The school I went to was definitely not set up with people like me in mind. My first years at the school were very tough, I was constantly bullied and victimised. I would sometimes come home from school and just start crying whilst trying to explain what happened. It was not the fact that I was a musician that made me a target, more the type of musician/person. Music was a big thing at the school at that time and many boys were involved. However, it was not because you were involved with music that made you a target for bullying, it was how much music meant to you. My life revolved around music, and when this is the case, it is only natural that you will have a different outlook on things from the vast majority of other people. It was the whole package that made me an excellent target for bullying, a package bound by my love and devotion to music. It was the constant support of many of the staff (both music and otherwise) who made it easier for me to cut my own path. I make particular mention once again of the then director of music and the headmaster at that time.

An interesting point to note is that I feel if I had only played guitar, there would not have been so many people joking about what I did. In my first two years at the school, whenever I performed in front of my peers I would be given a hard time mostly about my singing. When I arrived at the school my voice was not even beginning to 'break' and the fact that I was comfortable and willing to stand in front of a large group of students to sing and play my own compositions was too much for some people to handle; the more conviction one has, the more open that person is leaving themselves to others' victimising.

Senior years of schooling and beyond

By my senior years, many things had changed. My classmates were beginning to grow up and started to appreciate what I did. There was also a real shift in the attitude toward bullies. The boys who were bullies or still saw someone like me as an object of ridicule were generally looked down upon by the rest of the class. It was much easier to be so involved with music now; people really respected me for it. I have since had many wonderful opportunities and doors opened for me, and have been fortunate enough to perform with some of the best musicians around. I now plan to do an honours year specialising in performance and on completion of this am planning to continue further studies in both jazz and classical guitar in America.

About Brett

At the time of writing, Brett was 24 years old. He was born in Brisbane. He is the youngest of three in his family, with an older brother and an older sister. Brett attended one primary school and one secondary school. After completing undergraduate studies in business, he undertook studies in music. He is currently employed as a musician.

Brett's story

Early reflections and primary school days
I have always been surrounded by music in my life. My parents always encouraged us to take up music and to be involved in cultural activities.

The first years of school I spent most of my time playing sport and being an annoying little brat. I discovered that I could sing pretty well and at the age of six had my first starring role as an angel in the school musical. I remember being scared and wondering how my mates would react, but to my surprise the knocking and paying out did not last too long. This, I suppose, was my introduction to the world of music as an Australian male, a country that is predominantly concerned about sport.

Transition to high school
At the age of nine I attended an all-male school; this is where I was to stay until the end of Grade 12. When I first arrived the music department barely existed, but that was to change dramatically over the next eight years. I decided to take up a musical instrument; since I was very young I wanted to play the trombone so the trombone it was. In these years singing was always encouraged and I can never remember a time that I was not a part of a choir or a school musical.

Coping with adversity
During this time I can never really remember being picked upon because I was a musician; this is not to say it didn't happen to other people.

>>

I always had a great cross-section of mates who were involved heavily in other aspects of school life and I guess I looked upon my involvement in music as being my way of being involved in the life of the school. I also played sport but was never as good as some of my mates. I always found, and still do, that if you encourage your friends in whatever they do then they will encourage you in whatever you choose to do with your life. This is a sure way of finding out who your real friends are.

During my time in high school I developed a great love of music and it soon became my greatest concern in life. I probably didn't practise as much as I should have, but helping to develop a part of that school still to this day gives me much pride and satisfaction.

Senior years of schooling and beyond

After leaving school I studied business, majoring in accounting, but I soon discovered that this was not for me. I joined an amateur musical society and yet again a whole new world opened up. It was from here that I discovered the excitement of singing, acting and performing on stage in general. I discovered a whole new group of friends who were actually interested in what I was. This is an important part of life, if you can't find people who have the same interests as you then you will not get as far in life. If you don't have somebody who understands you and encourages you then the bar does not raise the extra step it should or could. I guess it's all about challenging yourself to be the best you can be at whatever you choose to do and friends and mates are an important part of this. You must have some sort of support structure set up in your life. This idea has helped me to achieve my goals in life.

As for being a male in the world of music in a country that loves sport more than anything else, I really have never had any major problems. Sure, you have your occasional yobbo idiot who gives you a hard time but it's people like that that drives me harder to convince people that music should be an important part of life.

There is one thing that you never realise about being a musician while you are at school: girls love it!!!!!!!!!!!!!

So what? Lessons from recent research and anecdotal accounts

The stories of Brian and Brett reveal much about the experience of adolescent music making in schools. Supportive parents in the early years, as revealed in Clare Hall's chapter, provide a considerable foundation for the years ahead.

Parents can:

- sing with children during infancy
- allow children to improvise singing and playing songs
- provide formal and informal opportunities to participate in music making
- be aware of the musical challenges of transition into adolescence years in instrument choice and voice change
- encourage students to continue participation through the middle years into early adulthood.

Schools have a significant role to play. Given that there are different models of schooling across the country, the transition to secondary school is managed in different ways. While middle schooling seems to provide the most supportive learning situation for students, schools have the opportunity to enhance student development.

Schools can:

- provide supportive environments for students
- facilitate a wide variety of formal and informal settings for learning
- increase awareness of factors that inhibit full participation
- invest in human and physical resources to support music education.

Almost without exception, Brian, Brett and many other boys attribute their involvement in music to one individual, often a teacher. The importance of teacher influence cannot be understated.

Teachers can:

- take a zero tolerance to bullying of any kind
- support students through the adolescent years, particularly in relation to voice change
- develop collegial approaches to the education of boys
- develop intra and inter-faculty strategies for the management of boys.

With the support of parents, schools and teachers, boys and men may still resist the opportunities at hand. Boys and men need to encourage each other, as peer mentoring can increase satisfaction and involvement in music.

Boys and men can:

- take advantage of opportunities on offer
- act as mentors and role models for students
- be aware that the middle years of schooling can be the most difficult
- positively engage with music through the lifespan.

A supportive environment in which parents, students, teachers and schools have a common focus is of importance, as Anita Collins pointed out in Chapter 3. Within these environments, role models from the ranks of teachers, peers and community representatives are *the most critical component* of all.

Endnotes

1   For a feminine–masculine continuum of musical instruments, see Harrison (2007).
2   Pseudonyms have been used throughout.

References

Adler, A. & Harrison, S. (2004). Swinging Back the Gender Pendulum: Addressing boys' needs in music education research and practice, in L. Bartel (ed.), *Research to Practice – A biennial series: Questioning the music education paradigm,* pp. 270–89, Toronto: Canadian Music Educators Association.

Ainley, J., Collins, C., Batten, M. & Getty, C. (1996). *Gender and School Education,* Melbourne: ACER Press.

Australian Bureau of Statistics (2006). *Survey of Children's Participation in Cultural and Leisure Activities,* Canberra: Australian Bureau of Statistics.

Black, C. (2004). The Arts in the Education of Boys, address to the Boys and Music Conference, November, Melbourne.

Bryce, J., Mendelovits, J., Beavis, A., McQueen, J. & Adams, I. (2004). *Evaluation of School-based Arts Education Programmes in Australian Schools,* Australian Council for Educational Research and Department of Education, Science and Training, http://www.dest.gov.au, accessed 25/01/2007.

Eccles, J., Barber, B. L., Stone, M. & Hunt. J. (2003). Extracurricular Activities and Adolescent Development, *Journal of Social Issues,* 59(4), pp. 865–89.

Fullarton, S., Walker, M., Ainley, J. & Hillman, K. (2003). *Longitudinal Surveys of Australian Youth Research Report 13: Patterns of participation in Year 12,* Melbourne: Australian Council for Educational Research.

Green, L. (1993). Music, Gender and Education: A report on some exploratory research, *British Journal of Music Education,* 10, pp. 219–53.

Green L. (1996). The Emergence of Gender as an Issue in Music Education, in C. Plummeridge (ed.), *Music Education: Trends and issues,* London: University of London Institute of Education.

Green, L. (2001). *How Popular Musicians Learn: A way ahead for music education*, Aldershot: Ashgate.

Harrison, S.D. (2001). Real Men Don't Sing. *Australian Voice, 11*, pp. 31–6.

Harrison, S.D. (2004). Engaging Boys – Overcoming stereotypes, *Choral Journal, 45*(2), pp. 25–9.

Harrison, S.D. (2007). Where Have the Boys Gone? The perennial problem of gendered participation in music, *British Journal of Music Education, 24*(3), pp. 267–80.

Hissey, M. (2004). A Cool Place to Be, *Music in Action, 1*(3), www.musicinaction.org.au, accessed 25/01/2008.

Marsh, H. & Kleitman, J. (2002). Extra Curricular School Activities: The good, the bad and the non linear, *Harvard Educational Review, 72*(4), pp. 464–514.

Martino, W. (1995). Gendered Learning Practices: Exploring the costs of hegemonic masculinity for girls and boys in schools, Proceedings of the Promoting Gender Equity conference, Canberra, 22–24 February, reproduced in *Gender Equity: A framework for Australian schools*, pp. 122–44.

Pascoe, R., Leong, S., MacCallum, J., Mackinlay, E., Marsh, K., Smith, B. et al. (2005). *National Review of School Music Education: Augmenting the diminished*, Canberra: Australian Government.

Paye, T. (2005). Instrumental Music: A challenge for boys, in J. Prideaux (ed.), *More Than Just Marks*, Melbourne: Pennon Publishing.

Pitts, S. (2005). *Valuing Music Participation*, Burlington, VT: Ashgate Publishing Co.

Plummer, D. (1999). *One of the Boys: Masculinity, homophobia and modern manhood*, New York: Harrington.

Rigby, K. (1997). What Children Tell Us About Bullying in Schools, *Children Australia, 22*(2), pp. 28–34.

Siebenaler, D. (2006). Factors that Predict Participation in Choral Music for High-school Students, *Research and Issues in Music Education, 4*(1), pp. 1–11.

Temmerman, N. (2007). Arts Education and its Contribution to the Development of Australia's Creative, Ideas Economy, University of Southern Queensland Professorial lecture, 5 June.

5 | The singing classroom: Singing in classroom music and its potential to transform school culture

ANTHONY YOUNG, St Laurence's College, Brisbane

This chapter examines the use of singing as the primary mode of instruction in the all-boys secondary school classroom. The place of singing within an aural-based curriculum framework is discussed; in particular, how logical sequencing of learning simultaneously benefits vocal development and the musical development of students in the early years of secondary school. A number of practical solutions are offered for assisting students with changing voices, as well as basic principles for voice training. With this foundation in the classroom program, a whole-school culture of singing can be created.

The context

I teach at a middle-class Christian Brothers day school for 1400 boys aged 10–17 years, having previously taught in a working-class, co-educational state high school (ages 12–17) for six years. Ten years ago, the school did not offer the state senior syllabus in music. Music was compulsory in the junior and the first year of middle school, but the middle-school elective classes were not healthy (six students in Year 9). There was a junior school choir (all unchanged voices) being well run, but there was no permanently rehearsing middle or upper-school choir. There was a single concert band and stage band, but neither was of a comparable standard to local state high schools. The strings program was tiny, but there was an excellent classical guitar program. Community singing by the whole college was restricted to the national anthem and the school song at assemblies. Singing at church services and at sporting occasions was dire.

Today, the school boasts five choirs, four concert bands, three big bands, a string orchestra, two classical guitar orchestras and a worship band. Half of the 1400-strong student cohort is involved in music on a weekly basis, and the whole school sings together at school events and liturgies. The school now achieves outstanding results in both senior music and music extension, with solid numbers in each class. There are two elective, middle-school music classes in each year level.

A number of factors combined to achieve this change: a supportive administration, including an open-minded director of music; collegial and well-trained music staff who were supportive of each other's endeavours and worked to enlarge the pool of musicians in the school; and liturgies provided times when 'full, active and conscious' participation in community singing was expected. These events enabled me to rehearse students in singing with a real context and purpose, and over years the sound of the school singing together has become a gift the students take with them through life. A key factor has been finding opportunities to make music and singing a part of the cultural ethos of the school. These experiences have ranged from forming an annual, week-long rock festival, organised, run and performed by the students, to providing singing workshops for the rugby teams, introducing them to the traditional songs and chants of the game.

However, my key concern in this chapter is to deal with the contribution of the classroom program to the singing in the school, and the contribution of singing to the intellectual development of the students.

From a practical standpoint, if you want something taken seriously in a school, it needs to happen during class time. Almost by definition, less-important things are 'co-curricular' and happen before and after school. In Queensland, rehearsals for ensembles, including choirs, are considered co-curricular activities. So-called 'classroom music' comprises musicology, composition and performance. High levels of skill are expected in musicology and composition, while performance material can be taken for assessment from the 'co-curricular' program (Queensland Studies Authority, 2004). This can emasculate the performance aspects of music in the classroom. Performing, and in particular, singing, can be sidelined with the best of academic intentions.

If we assume that the teacher wants students to be able to sing and wants schools to have a singing culture, it is a lost opportunity not to teach singing in the numerous hours given in many school timetables to classroom music. Enormous progress could be made at a national level if we all decided that our children would have basic singing skills by the time they finished compulsory music classes (in Queensland, generally the end of the first year of secondary school). Teachers who act on this decision create whole-school communities of singers within a few years. If we teach singing only to those who voluntarily come in their own time to sing in our ensembles, we condemn the rest of the school community to undertake the role of (sometimes hostile) observers, rather than empowered participators. We should sing in every music class.

When the concept of singing in every music class was first proposed to me, my predictable horrified reaction was 'when will I teach all the other stuff?' Over the years I have come to realise that I need to use singing to teach 'all the other stuff'.

My old teaching practice led to the sidelining of performance in class and resulted in musicology and composition being taught in terms of practice runs at the senior assessment. Unfortunately, in my experience, simply showing students the end product does not automatically give them skills to produce it. I have found that talking and reading about music history is simply not as effective as performing music with historical and stylistic accuracy. Composition exercises, even when assisted by music technology, are simply not as effective as vocal improvisation.

We need to develop in students the skills necessary to enable them to work successfully as musicologists, composers and performers. In my experience, particularly with boys, performance must be at the centre of the course, and within the area of performance, the voice is the key to developing the musical skills of students. Since changing my teaching approach, student results have improved to be among the best in the state and, far more importantly for me, the results of the 'ordinary' or 'not very musical' students have been excellent. I am most gratified when I see the so-called 'untalented' students become confident, practical, highly skilled musicians.

My curriculum uses an aural-based approach, in which all learning experiences – performing, reading, writing, composing and improvising – are prepared through audiation. The students need to be able to hear the sounds before they reproduce them through performing, reading or writing. As the most effective way for students to show me that they can hear the sounds is through singing, this is the primary mode of learning.

Concepts are taught in a logical sequence, which is both physically practical for changing-voice boys, and intellectually appropriate in terms of student development and syllabus demands. A small group of teachers in Queensland, influenced by the teachings of Zoltan Kodaly and by numerous researchers and teachers throughout the world, have developed this sequence into a kind of road map to musical mastery.

Students learn to approach new repertoire within an analytical framework, which provides a solid musicological basis for aesthetic, compositional and performance judgements later in the course.

The teacher can confidently say to the student 'I have a plan for you'. This approach also protects the subject music from the claim that music is intellectually lightweight and just a 'singalong'. Our subject is just as intellectually challenging as any other; we just teach in a far more practical and enjoyable fashion! Further information on this methodology can be found in Swinburne (1980) and Feierabend (1995).

Why place singing at the centre of the music classroom activities?

It's equitable. Apart from the few instances of students presenting with serious vocal health issues, all students possess a serviceable voice that can be used as an effective performance instrument for classroom instruction. Students who cannot sing need to be taught either the aural skills or the coordination skills that they lack. If the teacher has the training to teach these skills, every child has the potential to sing, and thereby participate fully in music. Accordingly, success is not determined by the ability of parents to buy equipment, but instead, by student endeavour.

Of course, not every child has the same initial aptitude, but great things can be achieved by students who work at it. One past student who could not match pitch in his first year of junior high school is now, as a result of his efforts, a fine musician, singer, saxophonist, music teacher and head of music in a school.

The focus on singing has not narrowed options for the students in the long term. We have graduates of the school music program who work in vocal and instrumental music, art music, jazz, folk and popular music, music production, music technology, composing, arranging and teaching. In addition, we have graduates who are lawyers, doctors, optometrists, businessmen, auctioneers, builders and pilots, among many other careers, who all can participate powerfully in music as players, singers and song writers. Not one graduate has told me he regretted being taught to sing and taught to think.

It enriches school culture. If you decide to ensure that almost all of your students learn to sing and value music by the end of compulsory music classes you can, after five years, bring about a powerful change in school culture. After five years almost every child in the secondary school will have ability and understanding in singing. This is an essential achievement.

Let us take a parallel: At my school, there has traditionally been a great deal of time and money put into ensuring that almost all of the students are competent rugby or soccer players. In addition to curriculum time spent in physical recreation classes, huge numbers of students are transported after school twice a week, to sports training grounds. This culminates in weekly matches against other schools on Saturdays. The students playing these games have a strong understanding and appreciation of the skills involved. Later, when they watch the game being played by the premier side (the first 15 or 11), they can tell, for example, whether a kick or tackle is worthy of applause or a cheer, because of their personal experience. Because of their own involvement in the activity, they have a certain ownership of it. They take pride in their own playing and appreciate the playing of others.

If you teach your school to sing, all of the students can similarly take pride in their own singing and appreciate the singing of others. Because of their own involvement in singing, they have a certain ownership of it. Students will take pride in the sound of their school singing, and will actually appreciate and care about how the premier choir of the school is performing. I knew I was getting somewhere when 'non-music' students started coming to me to request particular songs be used for school liturgies. It was a sign that they cared.

Admittedly, this approach is hard work for the teacher without the substantial infrastructure and support systems enjoyed by a number of sports. However, the alternative approach is dangerous. It may be easy to choose to teach those who are already talented or skilled, and to run a small 'elite' program, but when the teacher runs out of 'talented' students he or she is out of a job! Worse, small elite programs run the risk of having musicians perceived as a small minority of tall poppies ripe for persecution, stemming from a lack of shared understanding of their endeavours. I believe that for the health of musicians and music in general in our country, we need to create a situation whereby musicians are the happy, normal, accepted majority. Singing together will bring about this situation.

To apply this material to school ethos in general, the basic suggestion is to encourage boys to be multifaceted in their approach to male identity. It is great for a young man to see himself as a rugby player or soccer player *and* a singer. His identity could also comprise graphic artist, debater, actor, scientist, social scientist, writer, charity worker, brother and friend. Singing can be one of many activities that enable the student to find a sense of value and acceptance, first in the school culture and later in the wider community. A good boys' school should encourage this multifaceted view of male identity. If your school does not yet endorse this view, use singing to begin a change that is essential in the context of the scandalous adolescent male suicide rates in Australia. When we sing together we belong!

It efficiently creates skilled practical musicians. Singing as the basis of class work very efficiently enables the teacher to develop aural perception, literacy, harmony, improvisational skills, stylistic knowledge, composition and music history in the real context of music performed in class. Voice leading in harmony makes much more sense if you sing it. It seems fundamental that if you are writing a song, you should sing it and see if the melody works. However, in my childhood, both of these concepts were taught theoretically, with no reference to sound!

The application of singing to the teaching of instrumental music is also powerful. I am sure many have witnessed the blank stares of students when questioned after listening to an instrumental recording with no preparation. Students will analyse a rock song more effectively after singing (in solfa, notenames, timenames, from memory and with inner hearing) the riffs, the chord progressions and the melody. Similarly, a fugue is more fathomable if the students have memorised the subject and counter subject before listening, and have an internal knowledge, gained through singing harmonic progressions, of the harmonic structures. Of course, all of these musical elements can also be reinforced through playing on guitars, keyboards and strings, transposing onto woodwind and brass instruments, notating on computers and arranging using Garage Band™ software, but I maintain that internalising the music by singing and with inner hearing is core. If the student knows the material aurally and intellectually in time names and solfa, they are empowered to work with it on any device.

The advantages of this approach are that all students have the capacity to become practical, functional musicians. Classes become much more successful because the intellectual development of the students is achieved through practical means. A practical approach is bound to be more successful with boys. Freer (2007) found that 'adolescent boys need a great deal of physical activity and movement while learning, teachers need to channel this propensity into productive learning experiences rather than see it as a behavior problem' (p. 30).

Practical functional musicians are an asset to the musical life of the school and the community. It is wonderful to have classroom music students in your choir, band or rock group who can read music, sight sing, conduct and improvise. As a choral conductor, it is a boon to have a student in the second tenor section of a male choir who knows he has the sharpened 4th (*fi*), which will create a secondary dominant, which will lead a modulation to the dominant key. This singer will lead his section far more securely than a student with little musicianship who thinks he has memorised his part and that alone.

Some years ago, a student-run Ska band was rehearsing after school in the band room. The noise levels were ridiculous and the senior student who was attempting to run the band could not be heard over the din. He aurally worked out the backing figures for the trumpet, sax and trombone and communicated them across the room using Curwen hand signs. I don't know whether Curwen would have been amused, but I laughed to myself and felt justified in all that classroom singing and hand signing. They had taken the musical skills from the classroom and used them to enrich their own music.

Suggestions for successful classroom singing in a male context

Repertoire

Once you have decided you want to sing in class, you need to decide what to sing. In junior high, it is important to consider what boys, particularly those undergoing voice change, are physically capable of singing. Swanson (1960) found that untrained changing voices often have just less than an octave range and was 'amazed ... how few men's songs lie within the range' (p. 53). There is no point starting the course with music the students have no chance of mastering. Swanson (1960) advocates returning to very simple pitch-matching exercises to enable students with changing voices to gain control over their instrument and increase their range. Similarly, in my school we start with three-note 'do, re, mi' songs and progressively add notes to the repertoire as coordination improves. Introducing new notes progressively ensures that mastery of the vocal instrument is physically practical and promotes secure aural development.

There is also no point in trying to choose music that the students will already be familiar with or will like. In modern Australia it is almost guaranteed that every class will include a large number of different musical tastes and backgrounds. A piece that will be enjoyed by some students might be loathed by others. A piece might be moderately popular one year and passé the next.

I have found it better to choose music for its value in the progressive teaching of musical skills. It is better to ask 'what piece can I use to teach this idea?' than 'will they like this song?' In the first year of junior high school, we begin with phrase, beat, rhythm, 'do, re, mi', crotchet, quaver and crotchet rest. Accordingly, we begin with two-phrase songs using these musical elements. For students with no musical background, there is not time to comment on whether the song is likeable or not. They are challenged to work out how many phrases are in the song, how many beats are in each phrase, how many beats are in the song, how many different rhythms are in the song and how many different pitches. They are engaged in singing the song with Curwen hand-signs, notating the song on the staff, singing the song while walking the beat and clapping the rhythm, performing the song with inner hearing and performing the song at the keyboard.

Students who start the junior high course with more extensive musical background might claim they mastered the song and its musical elements in primary school. They are further challenged to sing and clap the song in canon, sing and play the song in canon, on keyboard or guitar, at a number of dynamics and tempi, transpose the song in a number of keys, compose a variant of the song within a set form, notate the song on computer in bass as well as treble clef, and arrange the song using a set range of timbres on a sequencer.

The advantage of this approach to repertoire selection is that the students understand that the songs are chosen with learning in mind. They want to know what new musical idea is represented in the song and what intellectual and practical challenges are present in the repertoire. Questions of like and dislike are replaced by questions of intellectual enquiry. Students are happy to sing the songs because they can sing them with success and because they are learning.

Intellectual involvement

The core of a teacher's job in the modern world is to train students to think. Students may appreciate you teaching them to sing or play or compose, but they will be far more grateful if you use singing, playing and composing to make them agile analysers, quick memorisers and logical problem solvers.

Lessons should be filled with achievable mental challenges that develop in complexity and challenge throughout the years of schooling. For example, earlier in the course the teacher might ask: 'Was there a new note in the song you just sang?' 'Can you write four bars of rhythm that complies with A, A^1, B, A^1 form?' 'Can you sing this simple canon in a pair?' 'Can you play on the keyboard with your right hand and hand sign in canon with your left?' At a higher level: 'You can now sing the theme of this two-part invention in solfa with hand signs, in note names and in time names from memory. I will play the piece. Close your

eyes and raise your right hand when you hear material from the theme.'
Or 'I will play you a chord progression we will use later this month,
close your eyes and show me hand signs of the bass line.' In the senior
school, 'You can now sing the gospel choral arrangement in solfa and
stylistically with the words. You have analysed by singing the chords of
the harmony. You have noticed the way the harmony is realised in the
vocal arrangement and the piano accompaniment. Make connections
between these musical elements and the social and cultural context of
the work'.

Appropriate and consistent voice training

If you want your school to sing, you need to decide that you will
teach every boy in compulsory music classes to do so. That means that
students who go on to elective music will be well prepared and students
who do not can still feel competent to participate in the community
singing of the school and in their lives.

In my experience, most opposition to singing comes from those who
can't. Welch (2000) complains that '[i]n the past, the labelling of children
into categories of singer/non-singer led to large groups of children being
denied structured singing activities'. Thus 'inadequate and/or inappro-
priate voice education, have consistently created (a) subclass of adults
who are embarrassed about their singing and this "fact" has become
part of their self-identity. To all intents and purposes they *are* singing
disabled, being products of flawed assumptions about human vocal
potential' (p. 713). Let us not add to this subclass! '(S)inging is a learned
behaviour and can be taught as a developmental skill' (Phillips &
Aitchison, 1997, p. 195).

The basics of good singing are fairly well established, and the
teacher needs to be able to 'teach the basics of great singing' (Barresi,
2000, p.25). Students need to develop control over posture, breath
management, onset of tone, resonance, passagio, diction, phrasing and
style. The challenge is to find enjoyable ways to continually reinforce
good basic technique. There is plenty of excellent material now
available on group vocal instruction, from which teachers can take
valuable activities. Frauke Haasemann and James Jordan's *Group Vocal
Technique* (1991) and Kenneth Phillips' *Teaching Kids to Sing* (1996) are
excellent resources. Wilson (1991) also has a pithy article on the issue,
which presents 'the basics' concisely.

For example, for breath and posture I have students stretch tall
with their hands above their heads. This should discourage clavicular
breathing. Breathe in and then let the air out without dropping the body.

This should give reasonably good posture and also the sensation of a low breath. Walking the beat while singing can often reconnect the singers' technique to the breath while simultaneously improving the students' sense of beat and rhythm.

The major challenge in this area is to have the goal of improving the singing consistently present and to work on the quality of the singing in every class and rehearsal. This sometimes means the groups cover less material, but it is worth it in the long run. They will sing better and the fewer pieces performed will sound much better. Again, the students will be grateful that they are learning more than just songs.

In spite of the teacher's best efforts, there are always a few students who seem unable to match pitch. If the student is vocally healthy, there are two basic reasons for pitch problems. First, the student may not have the aural perception to appreciate the pitches required. Second, the student may lack the physical coordination to match pitch.

The first challenge can be dealt with using the standard aural perception teaching, which is at the core of my curriculum. Students start by distinguishing 'high' from 'low' in two and three-note songs, and are asked to draw the pitch patterns of melodies in the air as they develop their aural perception. Later the students demonstrate their understanding by showing the hand signs of the notes they heard. The value of inner hearing and 'silent singing' cannot be overstressed in this context. If students silently sing a phrase before attempting it, it will usually be performed with better intonation. Johnson and Klonski (2003) describe this as 'subvocalisation', and quote Gordon on the centrality of singing in the development of audiation. 'A student must learn to sing or she (sic) will not learn to develop her tonal audiation' (p. 36). 'To be able to audiate a melody, a student must be able to sing, because when she (sic) engages in tonal audiation, she is unconsciously singing silently' (p. 37). There is a symbiotic relationship between the development of singing and the development of the aural skills necessary to audiate successfully.

The second challenge can be dealt with by some individual instruction. Welch (2000) advocates that the teacher start by singing 'sigh glides' with the student, progressing to 'sigh glides' that end on a certain pitch, and culminating in matching short-pitch patterns. These activities, with accurate, supportive teacher feedback (say 'that was closer' or 'a little higher', instead of 'that was wrong') should enable the student to connect what is happening physically with the sound that is being created. Once the student is able to match pitch fairly closely, the regular singing work of the class and choir should ensure satisfactory development.

Dealing with the voice change

It can be alarming for both teacher and student to work for years in the primary school to develop good singing skills, only to have totally unpredictable changes occur with the onset of puberty. It is not surprising that in Western culture, for almost 1500 years, conductors simply gave up and told students to rest their voices. Of course, this approach has now been discredited. Roe (1983) bluntly alleges that '[t]his process frequently smashes a voice into tiny pieces for life' (p. 180). Phillips (1996) states that '[b]y whatever means, adolescents must be kept singing!' (p. 76).

According to Roe (1983) 'all of the American plans agree that the young man may sing throughout the interval of time it takes for his voice to change' and that 'the voice will emerge from its period of transition with a wider range and a better quality than if it had not been used' (p. 180). Cooksey (2000) states that 'singing and speaking activities and training can be continued as long as efficient voice use and healthy management occur' (p. 730). Friar (1999) concurs, stating that '[t]oday's students can benefit from "singing through the change"' (p. 29).

Noel Ancell, Artistic Director of the Australian Boys Choral Institute, has an exercise which I have found excellent for improving the negotiation of the passagio.

Figure 5.1: Noel Ancell's passagio exercise (unpublished)

Source: Reproduced with permission of composer, conductor and teacher Noel Ancell,
Artistic Director of the Australian Boys Choral Institute.

Students need to understand the basics of why it is suddenly hard to sing in tune, and must be armed with knowledge about how their voices are developing so they have the courage to keep singing. Cooksey (2000) asks: 'Can an understanding and effective practice of healthy voice management during voice change better enable young men to withstand negative peer pressure regarding participation in singing activities?' He answers by suggesting that 'if adolescent voices were cultivated, using methodologies based on scientific findings, more young men would be encouraged to continue their participation in singing activities' (p. 736).

It is important that boys understand that their vocal mechanism is doubling in size and that the muscles operating that mechanism need to adjust to the change. Roe (1983) claims that 'the teacher must discuss the physiology of the voice with each class' (p. 178). This does not require lengthy and complicated anatomy lessons, but does suggest that students need a basic understanding of vocal function and development.

A difficulty for the teacher is that there is a range of approaches to singing through the voice change that are not congruent. Some approaches suit a very gradual development, while others seem designed for voices that seem to change very quickly (Roe, 1983; Cooksey, 2000; White & White, 2001).

Nevertheless, a number of classroom strategies can be applied with confidence. It is important to encourage students to continue to use head voice as well as developing their new lower notes. A number of students might notice a gap between the two registers, from where it is very difficult, if not impossible, to sing. Cooksey (2000) claims that:

> a large majority of boys can learn to sing fairly comfortably in the falsetto register ... physically efficient register transitions can be facilitated by vocalizing from the upper range downward if falsetto register can be produced with ease ... These register transition processes can produce a very consistent, efficiently produced tone throughout the singers' pitch range. (p. 828)

David Jorlett, Anton Armstrong and Jerry Blackstone also support the maintenance of the head voice, with Blackstone advocating extensive use of head voice for settling voices (personal observation). Jorlett uses a car gear change analogy in describing the change of adjustment from head voice to chest voice, which I have appropriated with success in class (personal observation).

Other learning experiences recommended by Cooksey (2000) include spoken sighs that glide smoothly from head voice to chest. These exercises also form an important part of the voice development regime advocated by Westminster Choir College (Haasemann & Jordan, 1991). Cooksey suggests that these be refined into descending five-note passages as voices develop. I have found these exercises to be very useful. Cooksey also recommends imitation of teacher modelled sounds, with various pitch inflections and voice qualities.

Untrained 'changing voice' boys tend to yell in chest voice if not corrected. This is not conducive to good progress. However, overly soft singing can sometimes result in unsupported vocal production, with incomplete closure of the vocal folds, leading to prematurely dry, tired voices. A teacher needs to develop an ear for a clean, healthy sound.

Roe (1983) advocates 'allowing the young man to sing out but not shout' and warns against 'continuous use of smooth, soft singing' (p. 175). He quotes Wilcox, who claims that 'the voice mechanism functions at its maximum efficiency ... when producing tones of considerable intensity (mezzo forte power)' and that the voice is under greater 'stress with a "soft tone"' (p. 183).

Kinaesthetic learning

Phillips (1996) states that 'a mixed modality of teaching/learning styles is best for classroom instruction if students are to be reached' (p. 28). Freer (2007) suggests that:

> ... young adolescents need a change of activity, focus or location in the room about every 12 or 13 minutes ... A meta-analysis of educational research concerning adolescent learners in five countries found males to be more kinesthetically and peer orientated than their female counterparts. (p. 30)

I tend to actually choreograph the space and use lots of movement in the learning, particularly in junior high lessons. Some phases will be in a circle on the floor, others at desks, others standing and others gathered at the board. In this way, the process of the different learning experiences is physically reinforced by students' location in the classroom.

Students will sing repertoire while simultaneously walking the beat, clapping the rhythm (either in time or in canon) and hand signing the pitch (either in time or in canon). Students might also sing a melody while hand signing the other part of a two-part piece. It is this internal awareness of other parts that is absolutely essential for good choral intonation and good musicianship in instrumental ensembles. Lessons and rehearsals should use movement to enhance the teaching, and cater for the natural learning propensities of boys. The beat and rhythm activities are also valuable in themselves for assisting adolescent students to 're-coordinate' awkward, rapidly growing bodies.

Singing and walking the beat or dancing can encourage better singing. There are plenty of circle dances that can be used effectively in a class context if performed with discipline and cultural sensitivity. Movement can encourage freer, better-supported vocal work. Often, movement will free up a stiffly held larynx or a tight-breath mechanism where no amount of direct instruction will. It is important, however, to ensure that the activities are musically done and not counter-productive.

Movement can also be very powerful in the teaching of vocal technique. Cooksey (2000) advocates using 'physical gestures that serve as a visual-kinesthetic metaphor for some aspect of the vocal skill being targeted' such as 'pretending to throw a Frisbee ... spreading open arms down and away with voicing or turning hands in rapid circles in front of the abdomen' to encourage active breath support and healthy voice use (p. 829). These approaches align with the work of the conductor Rodney Eichenberger (2001).

I rarely have a complete choral rehearsal with all singers continually on the risers. The rehearsal might start with the choir in a large circle for the warm up. My large (80 young men) choir walks the beat for the duration of the warm up so that they have a shared sense of tempo and sing in time. A canon might be sung to develop part independence, and all singers walk around the group attempting to hold their part while walking past other singers (beginning singers get to take a buddy to keep them on track). The choir will rehearse singing while processing on to the stage, and at the end of the rehearsal might actually perform on the risers. This varied use of space not only makes the rehearsal more interesting, it makes the singers less dependent on a predictable acoustic.

While the visual and aural learning modalities remain essential in good teaching, I suggest that a greater incorporation of kinaesethetic learning activities will positively influence male learning outcomes.

Learning environment

Research testifies to the restrictive views of masculinity present in some schools, and the way that 'physicality and athleticism', 'toughness and hardness' are the qualities that tend to be used to 'gain and establish peer group status' (Swain, 2003, p. 311). The music teacher must in some ways work in two directions simultaneously in order to deal with this cruel reality. Using the kinaesthetic activities described above can enable musical activities to involve the physicality and athleticism that can make it an acceptable representation of masculinity in the minds of the young men. Roe (1983) advises junior high school teachers to recruit athletes because of the 'prestige it gives to the music department' in the American context (p. 176). Harrison (2005) reports on the advantages of allying music and sport, but wisely cautions against an unreflective adoption of sporting concepts. He advocates the adoption of the positive aspects of sporting culture such as team work and reliability, while cautioning against a win-at-all-costs, competitive mentality.

Accordingly, the music teacher, while adopting an athletic approach to music making, must simultaneously work to ensure that the experience of music making is a safe, supportive one, where a 'personal best' is just as valuable as a 'winning' performance. A safe classroom environment is absolutely essential. Roe (1983) states that 'the teacher must handle emotional adjustments as well as the physical' and that 'young people tend to be somewhat cruel and unkind by nature. Those whose voices do not sound manly, or are unmanageable, are likely to be ribbed unmercifully' (p. 179). The teacher must be valiant in establishing expectations of mutual respect in the classroom. Joel (2006) is reassured by the fact that, 'in time, boys make the transformation into responsible, caring young men' (p. 57), but this transformation requires active nurturing and sometimes courageous policing on the part of the teacher.

Unexpected vocal events (my students call them 'blow outs') must be considered normal and not an excuse for ridicule. Voice training is like target practice (Thurman, 2000, p. 196) and changing voices often miss. Show them how to get closer to the target and they will try. Make vocal proficiency seem a mysterious and difficult achievement and boys will quickly give up. Remember, the greatest fear of any adolescent is to be humiliated in front of his peers. While individual singing is incredibly valuable, it must be implemented with care. Small-group singing enables the teacher to assess progress without singling students out. Form groups of voices at similar stages of change and enable students to realise that voice change does not always occur at the same rate within friendship groups. If a small group does something impressive, they will want to show off to the class. This will lead to individuals having the courage to perform confidently.

A number of writers (Swanson, 1960; White & White, 2001) recommend that in a mixed-gender situation, boys should be separated from girls when the voice change is at its most dramatic. In this way, the co-educational middle school would boast a boys' choir and a girls' choir. The co-educational music class might have girls on one side of the room, unchanged boys in the centre and changing voice boys on the other side. This is a practical measure which, in particular, ensures that boys are in groups singing the same octave when their coordination is at its most precarious.

Your attitude and approach

Barresi (2000) expects a great deal of teachers of adolescent males. They must be skilled at classroom management, well trained in voice change theory and vocal pedagogy in general. They must be good vocal models, with high technical, musical and practical skills, friendly, patient and good humoured. He expects good concert organisation, rehearsal planning and an ability to search at great length for appropriate repertoire (pp. 23–8). One wonders if any of us would fit his bill. I suggest that a more important and overarching qualification is to have a strong, ethical concern for the welfare and musical development of your students. Learn what and how to teach, and have confidence that what you are offering your students is worthwhile. If you continue to strive to develop vocal and musical confidence and competence in your students, you will, of necessity, and quite naturally, acquire the skills you require.

Conclusion

This chapter argues that singing should be a core activity in boys' general music classes. It deals with teaching methodologies, learning modes, school environment and the changing voice. It claims that voice-based classroom teaching can be intellectually challenging, equitable, enjoyable and culturally transforming. It supports Phillips' (1996) contention that singing is 'a basic means of human expression', 'a learned behaviour' and 'a complex art', which enables a student to 'learn about life' (pp. 105–6).

References

Barresi, A.L. (2000). The Successful Middle School Choral Teacher, *Music Educators Journal*, 86(4), pp. 23–8.

Cooksey, J. (2000). Voice Transformation in Male Adolescents, in L. Thurman and G. Welch (eds), *Bodymind and Voice: Foundations of voice education*, pp. 718–38, Iowa: National Center for Voice and Speech.

Eichenberger, R. (2001) *Enhancing Musicality Through Movement* [DVD], Santa Barbara: Santa Barbara Publishing.

Feierabend, J.M. (1995). *Conversational Solfege Level 1*, 2nd edn, Simsbury: First Steps in Music Inc.

Freer, P.K. (2007). Between Research and Practice: How choral music loses boys in the middle, *Music Educators' Journal*, 94(2), pp. 28–34.

Friar, K.K. (1999). Changing Voices, Changing Times, *Music Educators Journal*, 86(3), pp. 26–9.

Haasemann, F. & Jordan, J. (1991). *Group Vocal Technique*, Chapel Hill: Hinshaw Music Inc.

Harrison, S. (2005). Music Versus Sport: A new approach to scoring, *Australian Journal of Music Education*, 1, pp. 55–61.

Joel, R. (2006). The Boychoir Model: A perspective on retaining changed voices, *Choral Journal*, 46(10), pp. 57–9.

Johnson, E. & Klonski, E. (2003). Connecting the Inner Ear and the Voice, *Choral Journal*, 44(3), pp. 36–8.

Phillips, K. (1996). *Teaching Kids to Sing,* Belmont: Schirmer.

Phillips, K.H. & Aitchison, R.E. (1997). Effects of Psychomotor Instruction on Elementary General Music Students' Singing Performance, *Journal of Research in Music Education, 45*(2), pp. 185–96.

Queensland Studies Authority (2004). *Music Syllabus,* Brisbane: The State of Queensland, www.qsa.qld.edu.au/downloads/syllabus/snr_music_04_syll.pdf, accessed 18/08/2008.

Roe, P.F. (1983). *Choral Music Education,* Englewood Cliffs: Prentice Hall.

Swain, J. (2003). How Young Schoolboys Become Somebody: The role of the body in the construction of masculinity, *British Journal of Sociology of Education, 24*(3), pp. 299–314.

Swanson, F.J. (1960). When Voices Change: An experiment in junior high school music, *Music Educator, 46*(4), 50–6.

Swinburne, W.H. (1980). *The New Curwen Method: Book 1 tonic solfa class,* London: The Curwen Institute.

Thurman, L. (2000). Human Compatible Learning, in L. Thurman and G. Welch (eds), *Bodymind and Voice: Foundations of voice education,* pp. 188–301, Iowa: National Center for Voice and Speech.

Welch, G. (2000). The Developing Voice, in L. Thurman and G. Welch (eds), *Bodymind and Voice: Foundations of voice education,* pp. 704–17, Iowa: National Center for Voice and Speech.

White, C.D. & White, D.K. (2001). Commonsense Training for Changing Male Voices, *Music Educators Journal, 87*(6), pp. 39–43, 53.

Wilson, G.B. (1991). Three Rs for Vocal Skill Development in the Choral Rehearsal, *Music Educators Journal, 77*(7), pp. 42–6.

6 | Sharing music with Indigenous Australian boys

ROBERT SMITH, Director, Boys' Business project

When I first arrived in the Northern Territory over two decades ago, roughly a quarter of all students in Territory schools came from Indigenous Australian backgrounds. Today, their numbers exceed a third of the total school population. Projections for the next 20 years suggest that as many as half of our students will come from Indigenous Australian backgrounds and that a significant number of these will probably continue to live in remote communities. While most teachers in the Territory anticipate that there will be Indigenous Australian students in their classes, many recognise that it is not productive simply to 'stereotype' Indigenous Australian students, given that contemporary educational philosophy encourages teachers to acknowledge students as individual learners. This chapter reviews the music education strategies my music educator colleagues and I share with our male Indigenous Australian learners. While our engagement with such students does not necessarily give priority to their Indigenous Australian background, it does acknowledge that they are learners among other like learners, with particular individual learning needs dictated by circumstances and capacities for learning, not by perceived 'difference'. At the end of the day, our experience tells us that what works for Indigenous Australian boys usually works for most of our other music students.

Introduction

My initial reaction to the invitation to submit this chapter, relating my experiences and suggesting strategies for working in music with Indigenous Australian boys, was one of discomfiture. Could I, as a person whose primary socialisation and enculturation render me an alien intruder, be so presumptuous as to assume I know how to share educational knowledge that is a product of my worldview? Furthermore, how could I have the audacity to offer advice to others about working with Indigenous adolescent males, given my comparatively limited inter-action with them? The honest answer is that I could not, or at least not without reference to the insights both of fellow music educators who work closely with Indigenous boys and of the boys themselves. To do otherwise would be unforgivably arrogant and, equally, obtuse. Before I proceed to more musical matters I need to clarify my thinking about this overarching concern.

If my Aboriginal colleagues have a shared pet hate, it is in the assumption that others dare to speak on their behalf, which assumes their inability to speak for themselves. Perhaps this explains a wide-spread and negative response from Indigenous Australians to the recent 'intervention' in the Northern Territory (Wild & Anderson, 2007). It wasn't that none agreed there was an urgent need for action where the welfare of their children was concerned. It was an apparent lack of recognition of the need for Indigenous ownership of both the problem and the solutions. This, in turn, led many Indigenous Northern Territorians to interpret the intervention as a potential repetition of that scary paternalistic stuff that is still a potent and feared memory.

It is only through sharing sustained periods of time with Indigenous Australians that we are able to begin to gain some insight into their responses to the frequency of outsiders' decisions: decisions based on such assumptions and the hurtful outcomes thereof. Let me cite an example.

Working in an Indigenous community school, I noticed how reti-cent the local teachers were about speaking up at staff meetings. An Indigenous colleague – also an elder in the community – explained. 'You whitefellas love the sound of your own voices,' she said. 'You never know when to be quiet.'

I recalled a game I had played years before as a primary school student. This involved giving everyone five pebbles each. Every time we spoke we submitted a pebble. When our supply of pebbles was exhausted we could no longer contribute to a discussion or conversation.

I asked my colleague what she thought of this idea. She became so enthusiastic about it that she decided she would like to introduce it to the staff. With the principal's blessing she presented the idea and she and other local teachers distributed rations of pebbles to all participant staff before the next meeting proceeded. The process of that meeting ran along familiar lines. 'Whitefella' staff controlled the agenda until, quite unexpectedly, a significant number had no pebbles left. One of these people was still adamant that he had something to say. 'You can't speak any more; you've finished your pebbles!' my elder friend called almost stridently from her seat. Her Indigenous colleagues clapped gleefully.

From this moment, a remarkable change came over the meeting. Now, the local Indigenous staff took over and, for the very first time – possibly in some years – their voices and ideas dominated. And, not remarkably, some genuinely purposeful contributions relevant to community education and welfare were made that without the pebble strategy would never have been voiced.

I should add, germane to this chapter, that this strategy is a powerful tool for getting Indigenous boys to share their thinking.

A global village

Differences we may think we can identify as 'ethnic' are little more than cosmetic. Harth (1990) suggests that, by giving undue attention to these cosmetic differences and less to our essential sameness, we may be led to perceive these ethnic others as adversaries. So-called 'race' is nothing more than an extension of the notion of family. Despite sadly misguided propaganda to the contrary, we humans belong to a single race, and our mitochondrial diversity is extremely limited. 'Two gorillas dwelling in the same small West African woodland could quite easily be separated by a mitochondrial variation beyond that encompassing the entire human race. Within our own species, there is very little genetic variation at all' (Jones, 2001, p. 79).

Put another way, real human difference is largely cultural. Ominously, our global village, based as it is on a universal international culture, threatens the extinction of most minority cultures through cultural suppression. The world belongs to either of two camps: the one supporting tribalism and an affective worldview, the other the dominant West-centric camp, which has little interest in maintaining tribal worldviews, insisting those communities either participate or suffer cultural extinction.

West-centric music education can be expected to reflect such a worldview, empowering the mainstream at the expense of other educational participants. The so-called 'mainstream' may appear to prevail. However, the Australian population landscape comprises not just the mainstream, but diverse cultural communities, including proportionately large Indigenous Australian communities in the remoter regions. Surely then, given the significance to the Australian setting, it is critical that a 'both-ways' view of music learning pervades and drives music education in Australian settings. In this way, music education can embrace equal and genuinely inclusive participation by Indigenous and non-Indigenous students.

Both-ways education

Traditionally, Indigenous Australian society prioritised community and extended family rather than material values (Harris, 1987). Consequently, although Aboriginal parents expect West-centrically oriented schools to prepare their children for access to the contemporary 'mainstream' and thus its workplace, the community anticipates that it will itself take care of education that supports maintenance of its own cultural identity. As Beresford and Omaji (1996, pp. 12–13) argue, adaptation to a multicultural lifestyle can eventually be expected to erode and assimilate Indigenous Australian culture, lifestyle and values. 'It is culture that provides the tools for organising and understanding our world in communicable ways' (Bruner, 1996, p. 3).

This is the risk placed by West-centric schooling, with its indoor classrooms, arranged seats and desks, and middle-class expectations of behaviour and rigorous timelines. These and a plethora of other alien factors clandestinely impose institutionalised racism (Eckermann, 1994). As music education colleague Peter McMeel affirms: 'in one sense our approach needs to be different, but no different to mainstream. Experiences such as this do inform a renewed approach to the teaching of mainstream music' (personal communication, 2007).

Growing from a need to maintain their own identities, and simultaneously having to function effectively in mainstream settings, Indigenous Australians have evolved bi-cultural strategies that enable them freely to move in and out of different roles and sets of appropriate behaviours (Harris, 1990). Both-ways learning takes this notion of passing through a 'doorway between cultural domains' to that of the exchange of relevant knowledge and cultural experience (McConvell, 1994) naturally excluding sensitive areas of gender and protected philosophical ideas.

Both-ways learning is a critical driving force in our 'Boys' Business' program (Smith, 2005). Teaching should always seek to involve effective learning for both teacher and learner. It almost goes without saying that living life ought always to be a learning experience. I have learned much 'at the chalk-face', working both with teachers and students, as the following vignettes demonstrate.

Making music with a group of boys in a remote Northern Territory community I was pleasantly surprised to find that they apparently already knew the original song I was introducing. Past experience working with children in traditional Indigenous Australian settings had taught me not to waste time echo-singing new songs, but to plunge straight into them. This had proven far more effective and acceptable than squandering valuable time on explanations and drawn-out 'me-then-you' learning processes. 'So, who taught you this song?' I asked, thinking I might congratulate that teacher on their excellent choice – after all it was one of my very own! 'You did!' a chorus of male voices responded. As this was my first visit to this community I was astonished. 'But I've never been here before,' I said. 'When did I teach you the song?' Their confusion was greater even than mine. 'Now!' they exclaimed, giving me a collective look that suggested I needed help.

Increasingly, I use this approach with 'mainstream' boys. No echo-singing or repeated line; we simply sing straight into the new song. I like the way it grabs their complete attention because they need to be on-task for this approach to work. Another way to achieve appropriate and improved outcomes is to provide delivery in compatible learning environments. If at all possible, when I and colleagues are working with Indigenous Australian boys we prefer to take them out of doors. Invariably, this proves a popular, preferred and healthier alternative to working in a noisy and uncomfortable inside space. Obviously, too, having access to the invaluable assistance of local Indigenous Australian male teachers and support staff assists in creating more amenable social learning settings. As Allyson Mills, member of the famous Aboriginal family of singing sisters in Darwin, tells us, when Indigenous people are involved, activities that acknowledge culturally significant protocols can be chosen (Northern Territory Association for Drama in Education & Mills, 1996).

My own experiences affirm this. Given charge of music in a rural secondary school, I found the attendance of the students from a local Aboriginal community sporadic, to say the least. Often, the pattern would involve their turning up on and around 'pension day'. Urban myth had it that apparently the local office insisted that school attendance was a factor in the pay-out.

Considered from the cultural perspective of a West-centric musician, the school's new state-of-art performance suite was a wonderful setting for teaching music. It was an acoustic dream, sound-proofed so that outside sounds were negligible and consequently darkened with its minimum of external windows, heavy acoustic 'dampening' curtains and relatively subdued lighting. However, for these more traditionally oriented Aboriginal students, these very characteristics must have been anathema. On those rare occasions when they did attend they entered the music suite diffidently and appeared cowed by its alien environment.

I organised for an alternative timetable to be provided for these students. Organised around pension-day attendances, I would work only with these students, and we would use the open-stage space rather than the music suite for the lessons. Suddenly, the whole situation changed quite radically. We had to extend the new timetable to embrace other days because the students (and particularly boys) were turning up with greater frequency. Of course, at this point their only real interest in school was to be able to access the instruments. Yothu Yindi was rising to its star zenith across Australia and, increasingly, internationally, and the Warumpi Band was making its mark.

The snowball effect of getting these students to school was beginning to show up elsewhere. Conditions were set for their participation elsewhere in the curriculum, and teachers began to recognise the importance of creating learning settings more appropriate to the cultural environments of these students.

Learning in such both-ways settings ought to lead to greater and informed tolerance, valuing, sharing and understanding in diversity (Rizvi, 1994; Eckermann, 1994).

We sat in a semi-circle, six adolescent Aboriginal boys and I, each of us with an acoustic guitar at the ready. The guitars were brand new. I'd sat with the boys first and we'd tuned them together.

Very little talk ... focused on what I was doing ... listening, with me, for indications first of 'nearly-there' tuning for each string, from low to high E.

Then followed the fine tuning at the end that would enhance the sounds of our collective performance. The guitars – and their new strings – could be expected to lose pitch until they settled. However, I wasn't going to explain this. We'd learn experientially as we proceeded.

Significant hearing loss may be endemic in many remote com-munities, an outcome of inner-ear infections from the dust and wet that often prevail, but nevertheless the aural acuity of Indigenous musicians should never be underestimated (Ellis, 1985). Neither should their visual acuity. I am reminded that for many of these young men in 21st-century remote communities, hunting is still a regular focus of life, where all-seeing vision and analytical listening are critical. Both were crucial to the event in place in this learning environment, too.

Without discussion I began strumming one chord, A. A couple of the boys had done this before, but for the others this was a first-time event. I continued, strumming 16 beats, then changed to E. Sixteen more beats and back to A. Over and over for a few minutes, then introduced D. Same idea ... and in no time at all they were with me, changing chords accurately with correct intonation and obviously enjoying the challenge of anticipating and interpreting my changes exactly.

Now I structured the three chords into the familiar 12-bar blues pattern as they joined me without appearing to drop a beat. I sang old field blues I remembered, Elvis Presley favourites like 'Hound Dog' and some were able with relative ease not only to play but also to sing along. At no time was there any discussion. We were simply a group of men, very young and considerably older sharing the satisfaction of jamming together. Inevitably, an audience appeared. Two of the male Aboriginal staff picked up guitars, tuned them peremptorily and stood behind the boys to play along.

Issues

Certainly, there are many issues and challenges confronting contemporary Indigenous Australians, be they in the bush, in rural or in urban settings. By extension these must also confront Aboriginal boys. Many issues arise from the students' perceptions of themselves as marginalised, in a world where, increasingly, West-centric expectations drive learning agendas. In one way or another, these issues impact on music education.

Marginalisation inevitably leads to a gradual and increasing loss of personal and cultural self-esteem. With boys in particular, this marginalisation causes students to be more defensive, thus conflicts frequently arise. Initially, confrontations almost inevitably cause offence to be taken and, whether immediate or delayed, invariably result in physical or verbal invective. In marginalised communities, there are often unwanted realities that are very difficult to address. On a daily basis, sizeable numbers of the boys we work with are confronted with domestic violence, substance abuse, dysfunctional home life and, sadly, schools in which teachers still have middle-class expectations of students for whom these may be totally alien. Again, there is the looming reality that maintenance of their own cultural 'business' is increasingly under threat. Depending on their relevance to working in music with Indigenous Australian boys, I offer examples relating to some of these issues, discussing them in context.

Where gender is concerned, there are educators who believe that the differences between boys and girls are perceived rather than real, and work with both accordingly.

> 'It's a girl thing,' Skarre said. 'Girls like fussing. They like caring for somebody and feeling useful. Boys are into other things. Boys like stuff they can control. Like cars. Planning the design, constructing it, assembling it, influencing it and manipulating it. Girls have different values; they invest in caring for someone. And they're less afraid of failure.' (Fossum, 2007)

For me, while boys and girls have much in common, their differences are considerable. Without giving them due attention, we are bound to ignore what Baron-Cohen (2003) terms the 'essential difference'. The preceding quotation, extracted from Norwegian fiction, could be describing essential differences between girls and boys.

Because the focus of this book and this chapter is on boys, I have made little reference to girls. To their credit, I have also observed that adolescent Indigenous Australian girls also work effectively with music as a learning vehicle in our schools. There are both commonalities and differences in the way each gender group approaches music making. More to the point, because of cultural and social traditions, boys and girls live and learn separately across puberty. Tannen (1990) and Wood and Inman (1993) inform us that, universally '... research reveals that most girls and women operate from assumptions about communication and use rules for communicating that differ significantly from those endorsed by most boys and men' (cited in Wood, 1994, p. 157).

Gender becomes a critical issue with the onset of puberty; traditionally because of the sexual risks their immediacy might pose, adolescent boys learned separately from the girls. Hence, boys and girls assume they will engage with music making separately from each other. One music educator colleague makes much of this: 'I believe it is right to link the process of learning music to the rite of passage to adulthood for the Indigenous and other youth' (personal communication, Peter McMeel, 2007). Consider that boys' *perceived* behaviour too frequently leads to disproportionate attention in schools. Being a boy and being Indigenous exponentially increases the likelihood of negative attention from teachers.

The good news

Are Indigenous boys somehow different from other boys we work with? While it is important not to get hung up on difference, primary cultural and societal expectations do impact on the engagement of Indigenous Australian adolescent boys with many aspects of West-centric learning. For instance, because music is regarded as integral to living in Indigenous Australian settings, Indigenous Australian boys may be the most intuitively musical of those with whom I, and many of my music education colleagues, have ever worked.

Firstly and crucially, they learn instrumental and musical skills as though by 'magic'. This is a concept I discuss later in the chapter. As members of a society still grounded largely in hunting and gathering, their visual and aural acuity is phenomenal, and proves when acknowledged to be a powerful tool for music making. Once Aboriginal boys identify the task in hand, they are normally highly collaborative and follow through until it is completed to their satisfaction. As music education colleague Peter McMeel suggests, 'the Indigenous inspired collectivist approach to teaching and learning is something we need to exploit in our approaches to young Indigenous men' (personal communication, 2007). Applying these attributes to creating the music and lyrics of new songs seems almost universal among adolescent boys across community schools in the Northern Territory. When I asked colleagues for highlights of their interactions with these boys, invariably they waxed lyrical about song composition.

Here is perhaps one final but pertinent piece of positive information about Indigenous Australians and music. Such is their level of musicality that one notable researcher insists that Indigenous Australians hear and engage with music at a more sophisticated aesthetic and spiritual level than other Australians (Ellis, 1985).

Welcome to the family!

Questions about family and 'country' (that powerful, indefinable quality that Indigenous Australians themselves see as their critical connection with their land and thus each other and their world) are fraught with dangers related to sensitivity. The experiences that remote communities have had with well-intentioned anthropologists and researchers across recent years has often not been a happy one. Questions that mainstream people might consider casual and friendly can easily be interpreted as discourteously inquisitive. Such questions will not gain a response, either by pretending to ignore them or not to have heard.

Traditionally, Indigenous children learn in the company of familiar people. It is common practice in a community whose structure is that of an extended family for incoming mainstream teachers to be given a token 'skin-name'. This informs the locals (children and adults alike) of their adopted relationship to other community members. For example, my skin name in Arnhem Land encouraged me to examine my relationships with others, to check with whom I could and could not communicate, and to become part of a particular cohort of my peers.

If the boys don't like the adults they are working with, they may passively or even actively resist and ignore them. Possibly for these and other reasons, verbal communication can be constrained. Visual and aural cues work well. In the midst of an instrumental session the boys promptly acknowledge visual cues to stop, start, play faster, softer etc., and transgressors earn the displeasure of their cohort.

Culture and learning

No matter who we are, the expectations and protocols that drive our own cultural beliefs must impact on our perceptions of acceptable behaviour.

Historically West-centric learning grew from a tradition of distancing and, to an extent, abstracting the learning from the reality (Dewey, 1922). Real-life situations did not need to be enacted for learning to proceed, whereas traditional learning in Indigenous settings was experiential. On arrival in a music classroom they will expect to play whatever instruments are on display. Children learn best in settings that connect with their culture of primary socialisation; 'It is culture that provides the tools for organising and understanding our world in communicable ways' (Bruner, 1996, p. 3).

Some years ago, I was invited by an urban primary school music specialist to share *gamelan* music with her Year 6 class. Aware that children generally have short attention spans, I opened my presentation with a truncated introduction to *gamelan*, squeezing my explanation into a brief few minutes. Across that time the teacher managed to remove half a dozen Indigenous boys from the group. As she stood the seventh, I asked, as discreetly as the setting allowed, what they had done to cause her to take such a radical step.

She replied that she could see that they were distracted and were beginning to be disruptive. I must confess this was not what I had observed. Having worked over many years with boys in Indigenous and non-Indigenous settings, I viewed their apparent disinterest as actual engagement.

Learning in music challenges boys to combine the cognitive and psychomotor competencies of both sides of their bodies, and thus opposite hemispheres of their brains. The argument goes that, with a less efficient corpus callosum linking [cerebral] hemispheres, boys and men tend to default to one – the left hemisphere – and thus find multitasking very challenging. Learning in music may begin to address this challenge (Smith, 2006, p. 198).

Given my appreciation of their visual and aural acuity, I believed – and was proven correct when we began the practical application of the classroom activity a few minutes later – that they had taken in all they believed they needed to know and were ready earlier than the others might be to engage with the task. After an exciting session, probably made more so by their musicality and pleasure in the exercise, the students departed and I sat with the teacher in her classroom.

'I find those particular boys so difficult,' she confided. 'They always want to handle the instruments when they arrive in the room.' She continued, obviously upset. 'If I reprimand them they laugh and ignore my instructions. I don't know what to do with them so I often put them out of the room.'

I talked about working within an educational belief system that was able to give negative and positive behaviours appropriate hierarchical placement in our strategies. If as teachers we give our attention to the many positives that children contribute to any classroom activity and as little as we are able to minor transgressions – and for my money most of these so-called disciplinary violations are petty – it is 'amazing' how quickly even the worst transgressors come positively to the party! My experience is that boys from an Indigenous Australian background have such an inherent love of shared music making that they ought to be an asset in any classroom setting. It is simply a case of small compromise and understanding in our expectations of the modes of their engagement.

More recently, I was invited to work with a large group of some 80 middle-years boys in an interstate primary school. This school drew significant numbers from urban Indigenous communities. Prior to their arrival in the room, I addressed the teachers in attendance to explain critical aspects of my approach that would benefit by their indulgence. A significant aspect would be this notion of seeking and promoting positives to the exclusion of negatives. I asked that they not 'police' the boys, unless of course they regarded an infringement as seriously distracting. In fact, I urged, the best way to learn from this event was to participate 'as a boy!'

The boys arrived en masse and sat up close and in front of me on the floor. Without welcoming them I burst into my opening greeting echo song, encouraging them to copy me through hand gestures from the piano. Within no time they were all happily engaged, responding with much energy if not choral expertise. It quickly became apparent that the vocal leaders were a large and enthusiastic group of Indigenous boys whose singing could only be described as 'physical'. At this point, one of the senior staff approached the piano as we sang together.

'Is it all right if I remove some of the boys who are misbehaving?' she asked.

'No,' I replied, between words in the lyrics of the current song, 'Please DON'T!'

Apparently ignoring my plea, she proceeded into the centre of the most happily engaged group of participant Indigenous boys and took out three I had considered positively as the obvious stars and catalysts in this performance. I tried tactfully to catch her eye but she appeared not to notice and marched them out the door.

The deflation in the spirits of the remaining boys was palpable. I imagined they would now be extremely tentative about further lively engagement. However, boys being boys, they soon resumed with a high level of engagement and enthusiasm across the remainder of the hour, participating in a range of musical and related games activities with many teachers joining them on the floor.

Creating new music

Adolescent Indigenous Australians enthusiastically identify with new cultural heroes and role models in the comparatively recent phenomenon of nationally and internationally acclaimed Aboriginal musicians. What Yothu Yindi and the Warumpi Bands began in the 1980s flourishes as a renaissance of creative lyrics and songs that reflect contemporary living by Indigenous young people. Favoured genres may include those that are universal vehicles for marginalised youth, such as reggae and rap, but as creativity gains momentum Indigenous young people, particularly but not exclusively boys, are making new and increasingly exciting original music, matched by equally compelling lyrics. What wonderful learning opportunities the proliferation of youth music and bands across the Top End have provided as authentic catalysts to learning and teaching literacy, and a whole raft of other educational foci.

For many of my music education colleagues, this 'composition-revolution' is the highlight of shared work with Indigenous adolescents. In school after school across the Northern Territory, music teachers are finding that almost all they need do is provide the hardware and software resources and a collaborative learning environment for their Aboriginal students, and the students do the rest. The majority of students are so committed to the tasks of inventing, refining and performing new music that behavioural issues are generally minor or non-existent. As participants in a contemporary environment, they not only learn to create and refine but also to market the products of their industry. The advent of CD burning on laptop and desktop computers means that community schools become small music 'factories', manufacturing audio CDs and even video DVDs for local and even wider audiences. As a colleague told me:

> It is right for the Indigenous group to immediately create new musical works as part of the music education not least because: they need to establish their cultural identity as a priority; they will, in turn, fuel an engulfing passion to discover for themselves the many facets of beauty and truth. This in turn develops the foundation for all that is great about music education. (Music educator, Brisbane, 2007)

Music saves lives!

The famed Papunya-based Warumpi Band is now disbanded, and its beloved lead singer has passed away. It's too easy to think of community based bands as culturally parochial. Although based in the western desert township of Papunya, home also to the world-renowned Papunya Tula School of painters, its members travelled internationally. One of these, guitarist Sammy Butcher, reflected his worldliness and accompanying wisdom in his philosophical and philanthropic view of the world. I was privileged to meet Sammy on a consultancy visit to Papunya a number of years ago, soon after the band had disbanded for the very last time.

Sammy was in the process of forming a new Warumpi-style band. Significantly, he had decided to draw its membership not from the necessarily intellectually able young men in the community but, with great vision and empathy, from the township's significant and alienated petrol sniffers. Of course, many were too mentally inoperative to be able to learn music at the level required but, with a group of boys and young men who were still relatively competent but becoming increasingly addicted, he spent much of each day teaching them to play. Then, in rehearsals that the community could share, they would perform old and new music.

Sammy had no doubt, and I can only concur, that this was saving lives. Levels of self-executed harm, such as substance abuse and suicide, are of epidemic proportion across Indigenous community settings. Music offers one proven successful antidote. Sammy was not under any illusion that these adolescents and young men would all stop sniffing the deadly liquid, but under his tutelage the band appeared to be not only rehearsing and performing great and often original music, but also keeping many of these adolescents away from the abuse.

The outcomes of improved self-esteem and pride were evident in the way the boys presented themselves. Music, like sport and art, has repeatedly proven to be a life-saver for young men in Indigenous communities. It should be no surprise that a tribal society values affective and recreational means of learning and living. What is important to the case for improved educational outcomes for boys and young men, and of course all other learners in those settings, is that these are recognised as perfect vehicles for imparting all areas of learning, be these skills, knowledge or understanding.

The successful introduction of practice-based activities and other programs that impart useful knowledge and skills-based experiential learning, has been the result of agencies such as Ausmusic. The communal sharing, in so many ways a positive in an Indigenous worldview, can unfortunately have a negative side when it comes to maintaining the hardware necessary for contemporary music making. Consequently, these programs include units of work focused on managing bands and resources, and equipment maintenance. Increasingly, as young men learn that without care their beloved instruments, PA systems, computers and other pieces of technology will cease to function, they are becoming equally competent in their management and maintenance.

Because the ways in which Indigenous children learned in the past were often governed by life-sustaining needs such as the successful search for food, for shelter and the like, learning was experiential and recursive. When asked how they learned, I have heard children suggest that it was by 'magic'. A colleague tells how the boys and young men in his community would gather when the local band rehearsed. The notion of 'rehearsal' was not a formal one but rather a 'jam' session. At regular points in the performance any one of the audience might take over guitar or drums briefly and play along with the band. As the band played through its repertoire of songs, the audience visualised the chords and sequences they performed and committed these to memory. He asked the boys who were watching 'How do you know what to play when you take over?' The invariable answer was that they learned by magic.

Closing thoughts

I conclude with a series of questions I posed elsewhere (Smith, 2003). Then, and now, I believe these are pertinent to improving learning settings for Indigenous music students.

> Concerns about our notions of 'dialogue', often heavily imbued by our own unbending west-centricity without recognition of alternative protocols for discourse;
>
> Recurrently justified suspicions that our intentions are 'duplicitous';
>
> Using opportunities for 'collaboration among primary culture bearers';
>
> Address[ing] issues of inclusivity, access and equity for all students;
>
> '[D]isengagement of many boys with appropriate 'life journey' and high rates of adolescent male depression and suicide in this and other developed countries are cause for alarm.'

I conclude now as I concluded then:

Music as a medium for affirming disaffected middle-years boys in educational settings has a demonstrated place in rectifying some of this disaffection. In other settings those identified might well belong to other cohorts of learners. Serious changes may be required of our attitudes and approaches, rather than of theirs, if they are to be successfully included and affirmed in music education (Smith, 2003, pp. 276–7).

References

Baron-Cohen, S. (2003). *The Essential Difference: Male and female brains and the truth about autism*, London: Penguin.

Beresford, Q. & Omaji, P. (1996). *Rites of Passage: Aboriginal youth, crime and justice*, South Fremantle, WA: Fremantle Arts Centre Press.

Boyce-Tillman, J. (2000). *Constructing Musical Healing: The wounds that sing*, London: Jessica Kingsley Publishers.

Bruner, J. (1996). *The Culture of Education*, Cambridge, Mass.: Harvard University Press.

Dewey, J. (1922). *Human Nature and Conduct: An introduction to social psychology*, London: George Allen & Unwin.

Eckermann, A-K. (1994). *One Classroom, Many Cultures: Teaching strategies for culturally different children*, St Leonards, NSW: Allen & Unwin.

Ellis, C. J. (1985). *Aboriginal Music: Education for living*, St Lucia, Queensland: University of Queensland Press.

Fossum, K. (2007). *Black Seconds*. (C. Barslund, trans.), London: Harvill Secker.

Geary, D.C. (1998). *Male, Female: The evolution of human sex differences*, Washington, DC: American Psychological Association.

Harris, S. (1987). Aboriginal Learning Styles and Formal Schooling, in M. Christie, S. Harris & D. McClay (eds), *Teaching Aboriginal Children: Milingimbi and beyond*, Perth, WA: Institute of Applied Aboriginal Studies.

Harris, S. (1990). Walking Through Cultural Doors: Aborigines, communication, schooling and cultural continuity, in C. Hedrick & R. Holton (eds), *Cross-cultural Communication and Professional Education*, Flinders University, SA: The Centre for Multicultural Studies:.

Harth, E. (1990). *Dawn of a Millennium*, London: Penguin.

Jones, M. (2001). *The Molecule Hunt. How archaeologists are bringing the past back to life*, London: Penguin.

McConvell, P. (1994). Two-way Exchange and Language Maintenance in Aboriginal Schools, in D. Hartman & J. Henderson (eds), *Aboriginal Languages in Education*, Alice Springs, NT: IAD Press.

Northern Territory Association for Drama in Education and Mills, A. (1996). *Working with Ally – An Aboriginal performer's approach to teaching drama in high school*, A project by the NTADIE, Darwin, NT: NTADIE.

Rizvi, F. (1994). The Arts, Education and the Politics of Multiculturalism, in S. Gunew & F. Rizvi (eds), *Culture, Difference and the Arts*, St Leonards, NSW: Allen & Unwin.

Smith, R.G. (2003). Music – the hatter in the outback, in S. Leong (ed.), *Musicianship in the 21st Century: Issues, trends and possibilities*, pp. 276–7, Sydney: Australian Music Centre.

Smith, R.G. (2005). *Boys' Business – Tuning in to boys in the middle years using music & the arts*, Newcastle, NSW: Family Action Centre, University of Newcastle.

Smith, R.G. (2006). Boys' Business – Affirming middle years boys through music, in D. Hartman (ed.), *Educating Boys – The good news*, pp. 8–202, Callaghan, NSW: Family Action Centre, University of Newcastle.

Wild, R. & Anderson, P. (2007). *Ampe Akelyernemane Meke Mekarle 'Little Children are Sacred', In our Law children are very sacred because they carry the two spring wells of water from our country within them*, Report of the Northern Territory Board of Inquiry into the Protection of Aboriginal Children from Sexual Abuse, Darwin, NT: Northern Territory Government.

Wood, J.T. (1994). Gender, Communication, and Culture, in L.A. Samovar & R.E. Porter (eds), *Intercultural Communication*, p. 157, Belmont, Cal.: Wadsworth.

7 | 'Girls and boys come out to play': My journey in gender and education

KIRRALEE BALDOCK, Glossop High School, South Australia

In 2005, I commenced a journey in 'gender and education'. I felt challenged to understand how adolescent boys view life, and to encourage them to engage with education. With this focus in mind, I researched the latest theories in boys' education. Along the way I also gained a greater understanding of how girls learn. The results have transformed my worldview and positively influenced the way in which I teach and my students learn.

Developing an appreciation of the intricate differences between how boys and girls learn and introducing appropriate strategies in your classroom can bring about improvements in the vital areas of:

1   Quality teaching – developing teaching skills and understanding of boys' education, and extending repertoire of teaching strategies accordingly
2   Excellence in learning – providing an engaging, stimulating and flexible student-centred learning program, recognising that boys have specific learning and developmental needs
3   Engagement and wellbeing – providing a program that students enjoy, encouraging improved attendance, retention and engagement, with a focus on empowering boys.

My journey in gendered education began at Glossop High School's Middle Campus, located in the beautiful Riverland region, where I am the coordinator of the arts and health and physical education. I am also one of a team of two music teachers. The music program at our school is dynamic and diverse, with a strong band program. Our students participate in bands, such as class ensembles, the 'Middle School Band' and our feature performance band, 'The Glossop Groovers'. When my journey began, I loved my job and my school, but I was not satisfied that I was truly engaging all of my students. I could easily identify who my disengaged students were – mostly boys – but I could not identify with them personally at all.

Each lesson I would watch my girls come into class chatting and hugging each other – I could fully empathise with them. Who knew what gossip had occurred in the 80 minutes since they last caught up with each other? I found it easy to give them a reassuring smile and a gentle reminder to stop talking. The boys would come running in and give each other a punch or a 'wedgie', accompanied by unsavoury nicknames better saved for the footy change rooms, and I would feel the need to break up the mêlée. The boys would complain, 'Mrs B., it's just a game'. It didn't look like a game to me! I would inevitably attempt to resolve the problem, creating needless conflict between the students and myself. Such a negative start to a lesson was hardly fertile ground for developing positive relationships, communication and learning.

The catalyst for my inquiry into understanding how boys think and learn began in 2005, when my school launched an Enterprise Learning Program (ELP). The ELP aimed to improve learning outcomes for boys who were not achieving their full potential through mainstream schooling. As a consequence, one of our school priorities became engaging boys in their learning. As a female teacher, I felt obliged to try and understand how my boys think. I just did not see the world as they did, and I found that I was not respecting their worldview. In order to tailor my curriculum to the specific needs of my boys, I required a greater understanding of how they learn best. When the opportunity arose to apply for a 12-month Department of Education and Children's Services Middle Years Scholarship, I enthusiastically applied to study my combined interests of music education and boys' education. And so my journey continued ...

'Boys' Business', a music program designed by Northern Territory educator Dr Bob Smith (2005a and 2005b), intrigued me. I attended and enjoyed a training and development session he delivered in Adelaide (Smith, 2005c). 'Boys' Business' is built on the premise that all boys have an 'inner wild man', a natural aggressor with a survival instinct. Boys don't like to be confronted; it awakens their wild man and can accelerate to conflict unnecessarily. They go into survival mode, and the 'fight or flight' instinct engages. Angry or reluctant boys are not engaged learners – a familiar sounding scenario.

Having learned some of Bob Smith's tools, I began the steepest, most challenging and simultaneously the most enjoyable part of my journey as I put my new understandings into practice. Based on this approach, ideally the boys and girls would be taught separately. In reality, my environment, co-educational classes and timetables were restrictive. So I began to implement aspects of 'Boys' Business' in my co-educational Year 8 music and drama classes.

I introduced a series of games to allow the 'wild men' in my classroom the opportunity to play. It felt great to give the boys something fun they were allowed to do. I was also pleased that I was encouraging social collaboration. The games provided a medium for introducing equality and inclusiveness into my classroom, and encouraged team work, not competitiveness between individuals. My students designed a poster entitled 'activity of the week', and each week we learned a new game with which to begin the lesson. We attached the name of the game to the poster, so the students knew what to expect when they came to class. The students loved the games and the new structure of our lessons! They ensured they were punctual to class, because they did not want to miss out on the laughter and good fun at the start of each lesson. My lessons no longer commenced with a battle of wills, the wild men weren't being aggravated and our relationships were intact.

Familiar games such as 'Zip Zap Boing'[1] were received with appreciation. 'Boys' Business' also provided me with a musical repertoire of games centred on rhythm and beat. I found it difficult to sustain this level of fun for an entire lesson week after week – but starting each lesson in this way really helped to establish great relationships between the students and me, and I found they were much more accepting of academic rigour such as theory, history and listening. To my delight, I also learnt that my students, boys and girls, gained many new skills from the games – often lessons that I had not intended to teach. My students were engaging with education because they were deriving pleasure from it (see Appendix 7.1).

After my initial link with Bob Smith's work, I was thirsty to learn more. By coincidence, a music colleague from the Northern Territory Music School heard a CD of 'The Glossop Groovers' and invited us to Darwin so that his students could hear our band and participate in workshops with us. Here was an opportunity too good to miss, as it would also allow my students and me to meet and interact with some of the students Bob taught. But how could we possibly afford it? We put our collective wisdom together and devised a solution.

Our band members began by picking 200 bins of oranges for payment, over nine weekends. Combined with support, contributions and encouragement from our parents and community, we raised enough funds to travel to Darwin. A short time later, a colleague and I took 'The Glossop Groovers' to the Northern Territory, where we participated in a 'Boys' Business' workshop with Liz Veel at Wanguri Primary School and performed for a number of primary schools. The following year, I again headed north to visit Dr Smith in Alice Springs. We visited a range of primary schools and I observed and participated in his lessons.

Having travelled some distance, both in kilometres and my understanding of boys, I now steered my path in a new direction. Not wanting to neglect the wellbeing and education of the girls in my classroom, I attended a seminar by Dr Michael Nagel, Head of Middle Schooling at Forest Lake College in Queensland (see Nagel, 2005). I felt that I had balanced my inquiry by discovering how girls learn best. Equipped with new tools, I was soon back in the classroom. After a boisterous start to the lesson with a 'Boys' Business' game, it was almost unreasonable to expect students to sit down and participate in learning activities such as listening to a CD. Influenced by Dr Nagel, I now introduced 'quiet toys', such as slinkys, play dough and pipe cleaners.

My first experience of introducing my newly learnt techniques was such a powerful learning moment for me that I felt compelled to write the following reflection.

Year 8 music

Today is the big day! The slinkys are bought, the noodle sticks are safely wrapped in masking tape, the playdough is fresh and my Year 8s and I are primed for a musical adventure in gender. Today I'm going to introduce my class to Boys' Business. I intend to start with a game and then during the main body of the lesson implement a strategy of Dr Nagel's.

We started with a game of noodle sticks to the empowering theme of 'We Will Rock You'. This game involved choosing a partner and throwing noodle sticks to each other on the beat. It requires cooperation, coordination, concentration and rhythmic skills. It was a blast! I've never heard such laughter in my music room before. Not only were the noodle sticks moving, but whole bodies were grooving to the beat. A highlight was watching some of the boys 'air drumming' during the chorus. This prompted an impromptu 'air guitar' display during the guitar solo. All very fun for the performer and the audience as our 'guitarist' hopped, jumped and rolled his way down the aisle to claps and cheers from his peers.

How could the remainder of the lesson possibly top this? Would I really be able to have a serious music appreciation lesson now and keep

>>

their attention by playing them 'Peter and the Wolf', narrated by Dame Edna? Time for Dr Nagel's box of tricks!

We went into our 'listening' classroom and the students reluctantly sat in their seats behind their desks. Their eyes widened as I began putting slinkys, playdough and bubble pipes on the desks in front of them.

I explained the purpose of each of the 'toys' to them. As we listened to the CD, the slinkys and playdough could be played with if they like. They were for them. The bubbles had a very different purpose. They were for me. I acknowledged that I am often assessing them, but how often do they get a chance to assess me? I carefully explained that when they enjoyed something in class they were to show me I was doing a good job by blowing bubbles. It might be an activity or something I say. The bubbles would indicate a positive assessment of me.

I pushed play on the CD player and I learned what it means to take a risk in the classroom and to feel out of control. I also witnessed that boys and girls really act and learn differently. So what happened …?

The boys all sat at their desks, pounding the playdough flat as a pancake with their fists. They didn't speak to anyone. They didn't share their creations. They worked independently with a quiet determination to flatten the playdough as thin as a wafer. As the music progressed many of the boys were pounding their fists in time with the music. Even more amazingly (and beautiful for a music teacher to watch) as 'Peter's theme' recurred a few of the boys hummed along and rocked side to side with the music. None of the other students commented on this at all and the boys continued to safely express themselves.

Is this all beginning to sound a bit idyllic for music teachers everywhere?

Well, it might have been, were it not for the girls in my class. What a racket!

The girls were my bubble blowers. I'd love to be flattered and think I was doing a wonderful job as my assessment was literally sky-high. But soon the tables were drenched and one girl was on her hands and knees blowing bubbles across the carpet as they landed to see how far they would travel without bursting. Those using play dough were building intricate models of penguins and discussing the cuteness of them with friends. Another girl lay on her back on the floor and threw her slinky as far as she could – holding on to the other end. This was too irresistible for one sculptor, who caught one end of the slinky and the two of them attempted to see how fast the penguin could roll down the slinky tunnel.

>>

Oh no – three more tracks left on the CD. Can I bite my tongue for that long? Can I ignore my longing for control? Have all those years of behaviour management practice come to this? I know how to teach music history and listening, why don't I just cancel the crazy experiment now? My, haven't the tables turned! This is not how I expected this group of students to behave. Isn't it the boys who normally disrupt listening lessons? Don't the boys normally drive me to distraction as they play with the gadgets they've accumulated in their pencil cases? Aren't the girls supposed to sit quietly and soak up the culture? Can anyone actually hear the CD?

I'd prove to them that they can only learn when I feel in control of the class! A quick quiz, just to gently remind them of the virtues of listening. I'll be fair, they can assess the lesson, too.

Hang on, they don't look worried. Where's the panic usually associated with tests? They're all calm. They look confident. They pass their tests up on the way out the door and they're smiling. Now for the comments – 'Thanks for the lesson', 'That was fun', 'Can we start every lesson with a game?' Okay, that's nice qualitative assessment. I feel great, they look happy …

But now for the important data. The hard facts. These test results will prove that no learning actually occurred. Hang on, the average grade here is 90 per cent. Everyone's done really well. Was I the only one who couldn't concentrate today?

What a lesson. My boys focused, my girls multitasked. I felt a loss of control – but my students felt in control. My students were in control of their learning and while they were at it they taught me some lessons. These included learning that:

- I could be a risk taker.
- Students don't need to sit quietly to learn.
- Learning and playing can occur simultaneously.
- Top resources don't need to be expensive.
- What I see and hear on the outside isn't always a true picture of what's happening on the inside.
- Students can be responsible.
- My students learnt a new way to learn today.
- Boys and girls learn differently.
- I still have a lot to learn.

Having learnt the importance of play in education, I reached the final destination in my journey. I attended training in 'Rock and Water', a physical and social development program developed by Dutch educator Freerk Ykema (2002a). This cohered with my philosophy that positive interactions with other students and teachers are essential for students to maximise personal happiness and academic achievement. My research also taught me that boys benefit from time in single-gender classes. By gaining the support of my school administration team and core subject teachers, I was able to deliver the Rock and Water program in single-gender classes to all Year 8 and 9 students for one 30-minute lesson a week. Having watched boys playing games in the presence of girls, it was interesting to observe boys play in the absence of girls. I had seen boys lose a game deliberately rather than face the embarrassment of a legitimate loss in front of the girls. In the absence of girls there was a freedom in their movements, words, competitiveness and facial expressions. I was encouraged and overwhelmed by positive feedback from my students.

I have learnt so much during my journey. Here are some tips I've learnt and also some ideas you may like to try in your classroom next week.

Tips for working with boys

Be ...

- friendly
- brief – they don't like listening to long instructions and need tasks broken down into steps
- positive –- don't use put-downs
- willing to smile and laugh (with the boys – not at them!)
- patient
- consistent in behaviour management (across the school if possible)
- physical – they love to play!
- a good role-model – whenever possible, invite other adults into the class so they can watch how you interact
- creative
- a risk taker – it is better to try something and fail than to still be wondering if it would have worked; boys need to see us fail so that they can watch and learn how to deal with it
- an elder – introduce a 'rite of passage' to your students; one way we do this at my school is in the transition from Middle School Band to the 'Glossop Groovers'.

Tips for working with girls

Be ...

- equitable – share tasks and opportunities among boys and girls
- physical – they love to play!
- a good role model – make sure that every girl has a female to look up to at school
- an elder – introduce a 'rite of passage' to your students
- expectant of high academic achievement, participation and social maturity.

Five strategies to try next week

Monday

Introduce your class to a new game with noodle sticks. Begin each lesson of this week with this game.

Have students sitting in two rows, facing a partner. Each student holds two noodle sticks (You can buy these at Asian grocery stores for about $1 a pair. It's a really good idea to wrap masking tape around the pointy end to avoid injury! To the CD of Queen's 'We Will Rock You', play the game:

1   Verses: Bang sticks twice on ground and once together in time with the music.
2   Chorus (first time): Throw stick to your partner and catch the stick thrown to you – right hand to right hand. Try to keep the beat.
3   Chorus (second time): As above, but left hand to left hand.
4   Chorus (third time): Two hands together!
5   During the guitar solo, ask students to be air guitarists – I'm sure you will get at least one volunteer.

Tuesday

Surprise your class with a collection of 'allowed toys' on the desk during a quiet activity such as listening to music. Quiet toys such as playdough, pipe cleaners and slinkys are great. I wouldn't recommend blowing bubbles – I tried this once and it was very messy!

Wednesday

If possible, team-teach with another teacher, and divide the boys and girls into separate groups – even for just half an hour. Play some games that you would normally play with the whole class. Observe and discuss the differences. Ask students how they learn best and how they like to be assessed.

Thursday

Give students an opportunity to compliment each other. You could do this at the end of a game or activity by asking students to compliment other students in the class. For example: 'I like the way Adam kept the beat steady'. Everyone likes to feel positive and affirmed – someone might even compliment you!

Friday

Time for a new game? How about Wink Murder? Students sit in a circle and you choose a detective. The detective faces away from the class while you choose the murderer. Once chosen the detective stands in the centre of the circle. When the murderer winks at you, you must play dead. The detective's job is to identify the murderer. Three guesses is fair! My classes love dying dramatically – the louder the better. You can extend the game with more detectives and murderers.

In conclusion

In the future, I plan to implement more gender-specific activities in my classes. To engage students, boys *and* girls, it is important to craft specific activities for their individual needs. I think it would be wonderful for more students to be engaging with education in a positive manner. I believe it is essential for all teachers to step out of their comfort zone for the benefit of their students, and I intend to integrate the philosophies of what I have learnt in other learning areas. I would also like to campaign for more positive male role models in schools, as teachers and as mentors. Imagine a society in which the school is at the hub of the community, with community members wanting to mentor students in a positive way!

I have learnt many valuable lessons during my research journey. These lessons make me more relaxed and passionate about my teaching. Most critically, I have changed my beliefs about boys and my teaching practice. I have learnt that boys and girls learn differently, and that I need to use appropriate pedagogy to be an effective teacher. As a teacher I found I needed to take greater risks during lesson time and to give my students greater responsibility in the direction that lessons may take. I realised that what I see and hear on the outside isn't always a true picture of what's happening on the inside. I observed that students don't need to sit quietly in order to learn, and that learning and playing can occur simultaneously. I now understand that a positive and empathetic teacher attitude is just as significant as appropriate and varied classroom strategies to ensure student engagement and success. I have discovered that my worldview has a dramatic impact on my relationships with others. By allowing my worldview to be moulded by the lessons my students teach me, the impact on my teaching and the outcomes of their learning will be positive. Perhaps my greatest lesson was that I still have a lot to learn, and my journey has only just begun.

Endnote

1   The purpose of the party game Zip Zap Boing! is to make fellow players say the wrong thing (which ensures they are out of the game) and to be the last player remaining. The game starts when a signal is passed around a standing circle. You can only have a turn when the signal has been directed at you. If you have a go when you haven't received the signal, you are out, and you have to sit down. Further details and actions can be obtained from www.partyplan.co.uk/asp/game_293.asp?CategoryId=112.

Appendix 7.1

GAMES IN MUSIC: WHAT THE BOYS HAD TO SAY ... (2006)		
Positives	Negatives	Interesting
Talking	Don't like the game 'Honey Do You Love Me?'	Learnt new games
No written work	Some games were boring.	They are different to other games we play.
No homework	Some people wreck the game.	The rules
Fun		
They have weird names		
Getting out of written work		
BY PLAYING GAMES WE LEARNED ...		
<ul><li>to follow rules</li><li>to communicate with others</li><li>to keep eye-contact</li><li>new games</li><li>learning can be fun</li><li>how to be quiet</li><li>to make friends.</li></ul>		

GAMES IN MUSIC: WHAT THE GIRLS HAD TO SAY … (2006)		
Positives	Negatives	Interesting
Fun	People talking	Learning new things
'Honey Do You Love Me?'	'Zip zap boing'	Boys never try hard.
Girls always win.	Boring sometimes	
'Wink Murder' rocks	There are no really bad things.	
Fun, exciting and new	People deliberately getting out.	
Less time doing theory	'Squirt'	
'Wink Murder'		
We get to learn new games.		
'Bats & Caves'		

BY PLAYING GAMES WE LEARNED …

- to follow rules
- good listening skills
- communication skills
- to make eye-contact
- self-control
- that you can learn and play while still having fun
- there are different strategies for different games
- the names of people in our class and got to know them better
- to make new friends
- that games have a lot to do with music
- how to keep a beat
- to have fun without being naughty
- to cooperate with others
- to concentrate
- to be silent.

References

Nagel, M. (2005). Frogs and Snails and Puppy Dogs Tails: Just what are boys brains made of? *The Boys in Schools Bulletin, 8*(1), pp. 36–9.

Smith, R.G. (2005a). Boys' Business! Affirming middle years boys through music, *Music in Action, 3*(1), pp. 16–18.

Smith, R.G. (2005b). *Boys' Business: Tuning into boys in the middle years using music & the arts*, Newcastle: Family Action Centre, University of Newcastle.

Smith, R.G. (2005c). Boys' Business: Tuning into boys in the middle years using music and the arts [Staff development conference], Adelaide: St Peter's College.

Ykema, F. (2002a). *The Rock and Water Perspective*, Greenwood, WA: The Gadaku Institute.

Further reading

Ykema, F. (2002b). *Rock and Water: Skills for physical-social teaching with boys*, Greenwood, WA: The Gadaku Institute.

8 | Talking technology: Boys engaging in music in single-sex and co-educational environments

SCOTT ANTHONY MASON, All Saints Anglican School, Queensland

This chapter provides strategies for the equitable engagement of students of both sexes in the technology driven music education environment. Technology tends to be perceived as the domain of males in education. A primary concern of this chapter is the practical application and teaching strategies used in the delivery of music technology in the classroom. The chapter's focus is on how technology impacts the education of boys, through meaningful tasks. Through reflection on the recent literature, personal experiences and curriculum applications, it provides examples of how the author has used technology successfully in the classroom. The chapter concludes with a discussion of my future initiatives, together with suggestions for further engagement through technology in classrooms.

Technology in music education

Investigations into the use of technology in music education have experienced growth in the past 15 years. Webster (2002) gives an excellent review of the progress of music technology throughout the 20th century concluding that:

> It seems clear from these trends that information in the form of text, graphics, video, and sound will be moving to a digital format, rendered with smaller and more powerful machines, and used extensively by music teachers to assist children in understanding music by having them create music more interactively. (p. 38)

Williams and Webster (1999) have given specific details on the way in which technology can assist in bringing about approaches to music learning. More recently, Internet applications in music have been a focus (Bauer, 1999). In Australia, recent research on the use of technology as a tool within the music classroom claims that it 'enables students who are not able to engage with music in a traditional manner, to achieve quality learning' (Ballantyne & Harrison, 2005).

Meltzer (2001), Ohlenbusch (2001), and Bauer, Reese and McAllister (2003) have looked at aspects of music technology as it applies to pre-service music teachers, finding that teachers at this career stage express confidence in the use of computing. Experienced teachers, however, acknowledged the need for skills in managing technology as a significant aspect of teaching in which proficiency is required (Harrison, 2004). This echoes the findings of Peters (1984), who called for an understanding of hardware and software for effective teaching.

Gender and music technology

The interface of gender with music technology has been a feature of the more general research in this field, with the presumption that boys engage more frequently and more effectively with technology than girls. Green (1999) found that boys are much more interested in the realms of technology and popular music. Feminists have debated the extent to which technology can be exclusionary for women because of its construction as a masculine domain, emphasising 'masculine' characteristics of mastery, skill and control (Armstrong, 2001, p. 35). There is strong evidence to suggest that information technology has been stereotyped as a masculine subject in schools (Cole, Conlon, Jackson & Welch, 1994; Friedman, 1995; Frenkel, 1990; Ordige, 1996; Spertus, 1991). This stereotyping has some foundation in the research, but the specific nature of gendered use of technology is of greater concern. Problem solving and programming skills rate highly for boys in schools, while girls tend to use computers for word processing (Cooper & Weaver, 2003). Studies have demonstrated that boys were much more likely to investigate their way around new software to familiarise themselves with it (Friedman, 1995; Ordige, 1996), boys used music as a learning tool in informal environments and were more confident in using them (Comber, Hargreaves & Colley, 1997). McGregor and Mills (2006) argue that:

> *Pedagogical practices music teachers deploy in order to encourage boys'*
> *engagement with the subject take into account the cultural implications of*

globalisation, media and music technology and capitalise upon diversity
rather than participate in the reproduction of dominant constructions of
gender. (p. 221)

This said, practical application in the classroom, including teaching strategies associated with the use of this technology, remains largely unexplored. While there have been substantial studies on creative music making using technology, there are relatively few identifying the resources of research in practice and pupil consultation on teaching–learning strategies that use technology creatively (Burnard, 2007). The practical examples provided here aim to address these concerns. More than providing resources, the strategies and teaching examples are intended for direct use in the classroom.

One experience of information technology in the music classroom

I have recently moved to a co-educational environment having spent most of my teaching career in a single-sex boys' school. I have not observed any significant difference in the approach, attitude or interest level of boys in a single-sex setting, compared with that of boys in a co-educational school. My observations concur with much of the research described above:

- Boys demonstrate a preference for practical tasks in performing and composing music.
- In composition, they have a lot of creative ideas but have difficulty in organising their thoughts. They enjoy using computer software to do compositions but often want to skip the planning stage – developing ideas, considering structure, timbre and so on, and go straight to entering notes into the software. As a result, they often waste a lot of time and have difficulty getting started.
- Many boys have difficulty in working towards a due date. Providing interim due dates for different parts of activities, including requiring drafts, assists boys in structuring their approach to tasks.
- Boys approach the area of performance with gusto. They particularly enjoy group practical activities, though need guidance to target the musical elements. In the single-sex school, I found a significant number of boys tended to approach practical music making like they play sport – hard and fast!

My personal experiences as a school student also reflect those found in the literature. In the 1970s, when I attended school, the advent of the computer had little or no impact on my education. While I recall sitting a 'multiple choice' physics examination that required colouring in the correct answer on a computer card, and sitting in a language laboratory that utilised reel-to-reel tape decks, the use of technology to assist the delivery of curriculum was almost non-existent, and in music the only technology used was the stereo system.[1]

The music curriculum has remained largely unchanged since my time at school, with performance, historical and musical analysis and composition continuing to remain the focus of modern syllabi. Perhaps the significant change is that computer music software is now assisting teachers and students to achieve educational outcomes that we could have only dreamed of at school. From software that generates orchestral backings for performers to software that enables students to hear their compositions played on virtual instruments, the computer has opened up an endless world of possibilities for the education of music. A computer, however, is merely a tool to assist in the process of learning and presentation of student work. It is of paramount importance that the process of planning, structuring, developing and creativity is not left to chance now that computers enjoy such a high profile in education.

While music curricula across Australia have differing methods of assessment and curricular focus, the curricula are still generally based around performance, composition and musical theory and analysis. Teachers who have integrated technology into the music curriculum have probably favoured the dimension of composition, but there are possibilities within the other areas for introducing technology. Some alternatives could include the following.

Musical analysis
- Aural training software to develop students' inner hearing
- Internet-based applications, including video on demand, YouTube, Online metronomes, musical quizzes.

Performance
- Analysis of video recordings (both student and professional recordings)
- Midi-file accompaniments of classical repertoire
- Auto accompaniment programs, such as Band-in-a-Box, to teach improvisation in the jazz and rock genres.

Composition
- Notation and sequencing programs for scoring music
- Auto-accompaniment programs to enable students to hear styles of music and chord progressions
- Loop-based programs, such as Sony Acid, for students to develop compositional skills not involved in notation.

The teaching facilities

The teaching of music in schools provides significant challenges for the school administration in allocating suitable physical resources to cater for the various areas of the course. The most significant of these is having suitable areas for practical music making. Finding rooms other than the main teaching room can be an alternative, though quite frequently these rooms may need keyboard(s), drum kit and/or amplifiers. This may require some creative planning by the teacher, especially if the class contains a large number of students who play instruments most suitable for the rock genre.

In addition to the considerations for practical music-making facilities, having music technology integrated into the curriculum necessitates having sufficient access for students to undertake research, complete online listening, or aural training and composition tasks. While ideally one computer per student is required, any less than one computer per two students is unworkable. It is possible to split the class, with some students doing work on the computers and the remainder doing performance tasks, though the capacity of the teacher to provide feedback and to satisfy duty of care requirements for both groups of students (who may be working in different rooms) is compromised.

While it is significantly better to have a dedicated music computer laboratory setup (with midi keyboards attached) in the music classroom, it is not absolutely necessary to have this facility in order to begin introducing and integrating technology into the music curriculum. It is unlikely that the school administration would outlay the large funds (presently about $80,000) required to set up a 25-computer station classroom with all of the associated networking costs, physical hardware, computers, keyboards and software, as an initial step for technology integration into the music curriculum. The teacher would first need to demonstrate how they would use computer applications to assist student learning and produce outcomes in the music curriculum.

When I first used music technology in the classroom, I initially had four non-networked machines. While this was a good start to integrating technology in the curriculum, it was really only satisfactory for small classes. Initially, students used the music software for composition and ear training, and a number of CD-ROMs that targeted musical analysis. With large classes I booked general-purpose computing laboratories into which I had music software installed. While this provided challenges with access to headphones, no midi keyboards and proximity issues to the music department, it allowed the school's administration to witness a whole class of 25 boys meaningfully involved in music making on the computers.

As long as a music teacher has access to a computer laboratory (with sufficient computers), there is now some excellent freeware and shareware music software that enable integration of this technology into the curriculum without financial outlay, except for the time involved in the installation of software by the computer administrator in the school. It should be noted that some network administrators are concerned about installing free programs on the school network, due to the potential for conflicts with other software and also the potential for computer viruses hidden within the software.

Composition

The area of composition is undoubtedly the part of the music curriculum that has been assisted the most through the development of notation and sequencing software. Many music students (and music teachers, for that matter) do not have sufficient inner-musical hearing to really know what their compositions will sound like. Music software is certainly a godsend in improving this area. One of the dangers of composing using music computer software is that students often want to circumvent the compositional process. Developing motifs, considering the harmonic sequence, planning the structure of a piece, and so on is often a neglected aspect by students now that we have computers to help with the output of compositions. This problem is particularly evident when observing boys composing in lessons and when marking their final submissions. Boys often have wonderfully creative ideas but have difficulty in organising these ideas and planning on how to structure their music so that it sounds cohesive.

Before setting any composition task, I believe students need to develop a toolbox or scrapbook of rhythmic and melodic motifs, chord progressions and other ideas such as a drum pattern. This will enable students to come to the task with some 'musical scraps' that they can work with, manipulate and ultimately produce a worthwhile piece of music. The computer enables students to hear these ideas in real time, and reduces time in writing repetitive material.

A sample task

While there is no single, successful approach to teaching composition or planning, I use the following approach at the start of Year 11, when students elect to do the subject. I assume only basic previous knowledge, as some students may be performers who have not taken formal classroom music lessons previously. The task is:

Compose an original piece of at least 16 bars (maximum 32 bars) for 4 instruments/4 voices (or a combination of both) in any style or genre. Your final output will be in computer format using Sibelius. (Finn & Finn, n.d.)

Compositional guide provided to students

Pre-computer

1   Develop some motifs for your melody.
2   Experiment with chord progressions in conjunction with step 1.
3   Decide upon the form of your melody (binary, ternary).
4   Write your melody and chord progression. Words?
5   Give thought to established musical style or devise one of your own!
6   Decide on initial instrumentation (voice/instruments) * Hint: have some type of bass instrument. You can always change your instrumentation later.
7   In score format, write out a blank score (Score in C is probably the best approach):
    • Write in your melody. * Is it going to stay in one part or move around?
    • Write your chords above your lowest instrument.
    • Write in a bass part.
    • Sketch in harmony in vacant parts (just placing in semibreves for a whole bar if you are using one chord per bar, is one way to start).
8   Write inner parts:
    • Adapt your long notes to create more interest –
      Decide on texture.
      Use imitation/canon.
      Remember, you don't have to have all parts playing the whole time!

Computer

1   Input your piece into the computer.
2   Adapt your score (melody, bass part, inner parts).
3   Insert performance directions (phrasing, dynamics, articulations etc.).
4   Refine, refine, refine.

Ideally, students will see a number of successful compositions (some by professional composers, past students and the teacher) in the style and format that they have been set before they commence the task. Modelling by the teacher is an essential part of this process, though care needs to be taken not to give too much, as I have found that often students will reproduce the schema that has been demonstrated and therefore it can stifle originality.

When I asked a student about what he liked about using technology in music composition, he responded that:

It's a lot more efficient to be able to put in notes and not have to worry about drawing up staves and clefs and dealing with key signature. It also does quick transposition. The downside of composing using music software is that it's easy to forget the basic rules of writing music such as avoiding consecutive 5ths and that type of thing.

Creativity remains at the heart of writers' and composers' skills, and the medium through which we create and finally present our thoughts can only be enhanced by the accuracy of the computer. Computers allow us to make small changes without having to rewrite the entire work.

The two most commonly used proprietary software applications for notation in secondary schools are from the Finale Suite of programs and Sibelius. Both applications offer great advantages to students doing a traditional approach to composition, as they enable students to hear what they are composing using realistic virtual instruments, or satis-factory midi instruments using a standard computer sound card.

For boys, this new facility is particularly good, as I have found that only a small proportion of boys who have taken senior music over the past 20 years have keyboard skills of sufficient standard to play their compositions. The advent of this type of technology has greatly assisted boys' interest in the subject, and educational outcomes.

Choosing between the Finale Suite of programs and Sibelius requires significant investigation. The various Internet-based user groups for both programs provide reasons as to why one is better than the other. In reality, the teacher needs to try both programs to determine which one is most suitable for both their needs and those of their students. Both programs offer trial disks to enable the teacher to make an educated choice.

Software is likely to change through the life of this volume. At the time of writing, the Finale Suite includes three programs: Finale, Finale Print Music and Finale Notepad. Print Music is a cut-down version of the premier product Finale, and is most suitable in the school environment, at a reasonable cost per work station. It has most of the features of the full version necessary for education in the secondary school and, most importantly, the files are fully compatible with either Finale or Finale Notepad. Finale Notepad is an even cheaper option than Finale Print Music, and is ideal for students to download at home. Earlier versions of Finale Notepad were completely free; a small fee has since been introduced. The student can take home compositional work from school and work on the composition at home. The work saved can then be re-opened on the school system.

Finale Notepad does have some limitations, such as notes only being able to be entered using simple note entry (using the mouse or a connected midi controller) and having a maximum score of eight staves.

Recent additions to the software from the 2008 version onwards have allowed songs to be saved in both the native file format and in standard midi format, which allows the file to be opened by other software applications. This has been a welcome new feature of the software, which previously only allowed saving in the Finale format.

Sibelius is the other significant choice for proprietary notational software. Although I was originally a Finale user, I have recently changed to a school with an existing computer laboratory in which Sibelius was installed. I have found Sibelius to be a highly intuitive program to use, and students (and in particular boys) have found it an easier program to pick up and to use in composition tasks. Although it can save files (like Finale) in a variety of file formats, including the generic midi format, it does not have a free or cut-down version for students to work on at home. If the authors of Sibelius were to create a free version for student use (like Finale Notepad), this program would become even more appealing.

Anvil Studio (Willow Software, 1997) is an excellent freeware program that provides students with access to free compositional software at home or at school. It has the facility to save student work as a midi file, which can then be imported into other software programs. The Graphical User Interface for this program contains a realistic-looking piano keyboard, which is used to enter notes. The user needs to select the rhythmic value and then select the pitch from the piano keyboard. You can enter notes to produce chords. Although you cannot print a score using the free version of this software, it does have an excellent harmonise function, which can give students some possibilities on how to harmonise a melody in homophonic style.

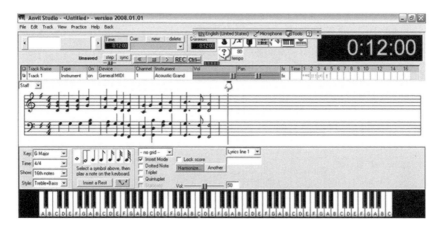

Figure 8.1: Anvil Studio auto harmonisation of 'Ode to Joy'

Accompaniment

Band-in-a-Box (Gannon, 1988) is an excellent program to supplement notational programs in the area of composition. It can also be used to provide accompaniments for songs in practical music making. The program can provide a rhythm section style of backing for any song in a popular, rock, latin or jazz style, and allow the user to change key, speed or style after inputting the chord progression. Entering chord progressions is done via the Qwerty keyboard, and the program can be tailored to suit songs with repeats, *del segnos* and first and second-time endings. Band-in-a-Box song files can be exported as midi files for use in programs such as Windows Media player or iTunes, and converted to .wav files for burning to CD. Songs exported as midi files can then be imported into notation programs such as Sibelius or Finale for further manipulation or analysis.

Students can gain a lot from analysing the walking bass line of a jazz piece, or the drum part in one of the latin styles. The use of Band-in-a-Box in composition can allow those students who approach composition initially from a chordal perspective to input the chords and create a skeleton for their composition, upon which they can create a melody and other parts.

Other applications

In addition to music notation software, sound manipulation software is also useful within the music classroom. Audacity is a free, digital audio-editing program that has many uses in the music classroom. It can import and export .wav, .mp3 and other raw audio files, and it can record from a microphone or line input. While it has many little gimmicks, such as changing the track speed, pitch, tempo and timbre through echoing, wah wah, and so on, it also has many educational uses. Here are some of the purposes for which I use this program in the classroom:

- Importing CD wave file recordings and cutting out sections to create excerpts for students to study.
- Preparing excerpts for examinations.
- Importing student compositions for them to record a voice-over, explaining what their composition is about (in real time), or how they have constructed the piece.
- Converting wave files to mp3 to reduce size for transmission over the school intranet.
- Trimming portions of work to fit with video footage.

A number of freeware, shareware programs and programs provided with operating systems are also particularly useful in the music classroom.

Listed below are a number of these programs and some handy features that I use:

- Windows Media Player. While most people would be familiar with the basic features of this program, one handy feature for students who have midi-file accompaniments to solo repertoire is that Windows Media Player can vary the speed of midi files. This is done via the following menu structure: View>Enhancements>Play Speed Settings.
- Windows Media Encoder is a free download from Microsoft and is useful to do screen capture in real time. This program enables you to create your own video tutorials for doing particular tasks in a computer application. With the addition of a microphone you can do a voice-over while you demonstrate a computer process. You can save the file in a variety of formats to either burn to disc or place on the Internet.
- Magic DVD Ripper (Magic DVD Software Inc.,) allows the user to cut a portion of footage from a commercial DVD and export it in a variety of video formats. I developed a compositional task in a unit on film music that required students to compose music to one minute of film. Students were able to cut the portion of film from the DVD and save it in wmv (Windows Media Video) format and import it into Sibelius. Sibelius works very well, allowing the user to create 'hit' points and alter the speed of music to fit with the film. Magic DVD Ripper has a free trial period.
- Windows Movie Maker is a very simple program, which students use to join their exported music file from Sibelius with their movie clip for final export.
- Audio Grabber (Franck, n.d.) is an excellent freeware program that can extract sound files into their native format from a music CD. These extract files can then be loaded into Audacity (Mazzoni & Dannenberg, 1989) for further manipulation and conversion.

Internet use

The Internet is a wonderful (and still perhaps underutilised) resource for music educators. There are many sites from which teachers can download sheet music in a pdf format and sound recordings in a variety of file formats, free of charge or for a nominal yearly fee.

Some of the sites I use to obtain classical music scores and sound files are listed here:

- Classical Music Archives: www.classicalarchives.com – five free midi files per day of well-known classics; subscribers can download mp3 files for a small yearly fee.
- Choral Public Domain Library (CPDL): www.cpdl.org contains choral music in pdf format, with some files in Sibelius and Finale.

- International Music Score Library Project: www.imslp.org is similar to CPDL and contains pdf files of instrumental works.
- IMA: Werner Icking Music Archive: http://icking-music-archive.org.
- Sheet Music Archive: www.sheetmusicarchive.net.

YouTube (www.youtube.com) is a relatively new but fantastic Internet resource for musical analysis. Although the visual and audio quality of the performances (due to the file type required for video streaming) is not as good as that of commercial DVDs, the educational benefits of viewing an array of music far outweigh this problem. Many video recordings are available of current artists in all musical genres, along with archival footage of some of the performers of yesteryear, and it's free! Analysis of performers through audiovisual viewing is significantly better than just listening to sound recordings with a score, due to the increased level of sensory engagement. It is possible to save the link (URL) to the YouTube video onto a school intranet or PowerPoint file for viewing on demand. Boys, in particular, are significantly more focused when the learning involves both aural and visual analysis.

Student outcomes through use of computer software

There is no doubt that the computer is now an essential part of the modern teacher's tool box, and that failure to integrate technology into the music curriculum is to deprive students of something that is now a part of their way of life. Enhancing the curriculum through the use of technology can be daunting for those teachers not versed in the area. If a universal aspiration of all music educators is to improve the quality of musical learning and its relevance to the young learner, then we need to rethink how a teacher's capacity to effectively use technology matches the pupils' learning needs. (Burnard, 2007). Through a little experimentation and a willingness to take on the challenge, learning a new tool with the students can be rewarding for both the teacher and the students, and will undoubtedly raise the profile of the teacher in the student's eyes. As students progress through the higher years of school, the focus in education should move from teacher-directed learning to student-focused learning. The teacher learning along with the students is an important paradigm. Ultimately, we facilitate students to be life-long learners.

By their nature, students (and in particular boys) are prepared to take more risks and are not worried about failure in the same way that adults are. While teachers often look through help menus and manuals to solve problems, boys enjoy experimenting through trial and error, and often discover alternative methods of achieving outcomes. Boys love being able to show a teacher a trick or two, especially in the area of technology. View this as a positive, and something that helps you and raises the self-esteem of the student. It's rare to hear students gloating that they knew how to do something and the teacher didn't. The more likely case is that the boy feels good that he was able to share something with a teacher or another student.

One of the dangers of using technology in the classroom is that students often want to cut corners when it comes to education, and the computer can often exacerbate this problem. While it is unlikely that the process involved in practical music making can be exploited by the computer, the use of computers in the area of composition can be problematic. Boys often want to get the finished article out straight away, without worrying about the construction and development of their ideas through refinement. The challenge for the teacher is to ensure that boys follow a process and use the computer to assist the student in the task.

The attraction to plagiarise (both text and sound files) from the Internet is a greater problem. Students can download midi files of composers, make a small adaptation in a notation program and attempt to pass someone else's work as their own. The key in detection is to look out for the atypical degree of sophistication in the work, an instrument perhaps in a usual key, or an almost-completed composition appearing without you seeing the process through drafting. I detected an example of this quite recently when, after some badgering, a student reluctantly showed me his final composition draft. At a first glance, the composition looked highly professional, with good structure and cohesive writing. On closer inspection I noticed the melody and harmonic structure sounded somewhat familiar to me, and that instrumentation included a part for Trumpet in D. The student had downloaded Mendelssohn's Hebrides Overture and changed the melody.

Conclusion

Whether it is the Play Station, X-Box or Sibelius notational software, boys love engaging in technology, and find it an essential part of work and play. The challenge for the teacher in the 21st century is to harness boys' tactile approach to learning through meaningful tasks that utilise technology, yet at the same time provide the necessary structure in their education that boys really need.

The challenge with the technology is to facilitate better outcomes for the students without sacrificing the learning process or missing essential elements. A computer should be used as a tool to supplement the learning process and provide students with new ways of achieving skills and enhancing their output.

Technology can be easily introduced into the music curriculum, with little to no budget, through the use of freeware or shareware music programs that can initially be installed on computers in multipurpose laboratories. Proprietary software programs allow greater functionality and flexibility, and can be utilised when finances become available.

Technology in music, when used effectively, can be incorporated and can enhance the delivery of the subject in every area of the curriculum. Notational programs can assist students in the compositional area by allowing them to hear what they write, while aural training programs can be used to develop students' skills in inner hearing. Auto-accompaniment programs can be used to teach students improvisation, or to create backings to their songs.

Computers and other peripherals, such as Datashows and Smart Boards, will undoubtedly continue to proliferate in schools. At the same time, the proprietary software programs will continue to be updated, with improved functionality and ease of use each year, and new and exciting freeware and shareware programs will become available. The challenge for the music educator is to learn how to use the various pieces of software to enhance student learning, and to update their own skills in order to cope with this new technology. As a new generation of teacher graduates (who are more IT savvy) enter the profession and are responsible for writing curriculum documents and work programs, teachers who began teaching before the widespread implementation of technology will be able to adopt some of these new processes and initiatives.

In addition to the use of music technology in the composition and practical areas of music, there are a number of other potential applications:

- Using the plethora of resources (some discovered and others not yet) on the Internet in the music classroom. There are a lot of worksheets, sound files and other resources that other educators have put together to assist the delivery of music in the school environment.
- Developing structured activities, using the software that is currently available.
- Developing web-based tasks that allow greater student interaction in regard to musical analysis.

There is a movement in music education that views as unnecessary and potentially obsolete traditional approaches to composition involving techniques that produce printed scores, and views the production of songs based on loop-based structures as the new direction for music curriculum in schools. It is my hope that this does not continue to be the pattern, and that the computer is used to further enhance traditional methods of music making and to stimulate creativity in the child.

Endnote

1 See Webster (2002) for a short history of the use of information technology in music since the 1970s.

References

Armstrong, V. (2001). Theorizing Gender and Musical Composition in the Computerized Classroom, *Women: A Cultural Review, 12*(1), pp. 35–43.

Ballantyne J. & Harrison S. (2005). Research Directions: Gender, technology and engagement in music, In P. DeVries (ed.), *Proceedings from the 27th Australian Association for Research in Music Education Conference*, pp. 9–14, Melbourne: Australian Association for Research in Music Education.

Bauer, W.I. (1999). Music Educators and the Internet: *Contributions to Music Education, 26*, pp. 51–63, http://www.apple.com/education/planning/profdev/index4.html, accessed 8/02/2008.

Bauer, W.I. (2003). Gender Differences and the Computer Self-efficacy of Pre-service Music Teachers, *Journal of Technology in Music Learning, 2*(1), pp. 9–15.

Bauer, W.I., Reese, S. & McAllister, P.A. (2003). Transforming Music Teaching Via Technology: The role of professional development, *Journal of Research in Music Education, 51*(4), p. 289.

Burnard, P. (2007). Reframing Creativity and Technology: Promoting pedagogic change in music education, *Journal of Music, Technology and Education, 1*(1), pp. 44–7.

Cole, A., Conlon, T., Jackson, S. & Welch, D. (1994). Information Technology and Gender. Problems and proposals, *Gender and Education, 6*(1), pp. 77–85.

Colley, C. & Comber, A. (2003). Age and Gender Differences in Computer Use and Attitudes Among Secondary School Students: What has changed? *Educational Research, 45*(2), pp. 155–65.

Comber, A., Hargreaves, D. & Colley C. (1993). Girls, Boys and Technology in Music. *British Journal of Music Education 10*(2), pp. 123–34.

Comber, A., Hargreaves, D. & Colley C. (1997). IT and Music Education. *British Journal of Music Education, 14*(2), pp. 119–27.

Cooper, J. & Weaver, K. (2003). *Gender and Computers: Understanding the digital divide*, Mahwah, NJ: Lawrence Erlbaum Associates.

Finn, B. & Finn, J. Sibelius (Version 5) [Computer Software], UK, Avid Technology Inc.

Franck, J. (n.d.). Audio Grabber (Version 1.8.3) [Computer Software], http://www.audiograbber.com-us.net, accessed 18/02/2007.

Frenkel, A. (1990). Women and Computing. *Communications of the ACM, 33*(11), pp. 34–47, http://www.cpsr.org/cpsr/gender/frenkel. cacm.womcomp, accessed 7/02/2008.

Friedman, T. (1995). Making Sense of Software: Computer games and interactive textuality, in S.G. Jones (ed.), *Cybersociety Computer-Mediated Communication and Community,* pp. 73-89, Thousand Oaks: Sage.

Gannon, P. (1988). Band-in-a-Box [Computer Software], Victoria, B.C.: PG Music.

Green, L. (1999). Research in the Sociology of Music Education: Some introductory concepts, *Music Education Research, 1*(2), pp. 159–70.

Harrison, S.D. (2004). Identities of Music Teachers in Australia: A pilot study, in M. Chaseling (ed.), *Proceedings of Australian Association for Research in Music Education Conference,* pp. 198-206, Gold Coast: Australian Association for Research in Music Education.

Magic DVD Software, Inc. Magic DVD Ripper (Version 5.0.1) [Computer Software], http://www.magicdvdripper.com/, accessed 4/07/2007.

Mazzoni, D. & Dannenberg, R. (1989). Audacity (Version 1.2.6) [Computer Software], http://audacity.sourceforge.net/, accessed 22/02/2008.

McGregor, G. & Mills, M. (2006). Boys and Music Education: *RMXing the curriculum, Pedagogy, Culture and Society, 14(2),* pp. 21–233.

Meltzer, J. (2001). A Survey to Assess the Technology Literacy of Undergraduate Music Majors at Big-10 Universities: Implications for undergraduate courses in music education technology, unpublished doctoral dissertation, University of Illinois at Urbana-Champaign.

Ohlenbusch, G. (2001). A Study of the Use of Technology Applications by Texas Music Educators and the Relevance to Undergraduate Music Education Curriculum, unpublished doctoral dissertation, Winchester, VA: Shenandoah Conservatory.

Ordige, I. (1996). Attracting Girls to IT. NCET, Information Sheet, http://www.becta.org.uk/info-sheets/gender.html, accessed 22/02/2008.

Peters, G.D. (1984). Teacher Training and High Technology, *Music Educators Journal*, *70*(5), pp. 35–9.

Spertus, E. (1991). Why Are There So Many Female Computer Scientists?   http://www.ai.mit.edu/people/ellens/Gender/pap/pap.html, accessed 7/02/2008.

Webster, P. (2002). Historical Perspectives on Technology and Music, *Music Educators Journal*, *89*(1), pp. 38–43, 54.

Williams, D.B., & Webster, P.R. (1999). *Experiencing Music Technology* (2nd edn), New York: Schirmer.

Willow Software (1997). *Anvil Studio* (Version 2007.12.01) [Computer Software], http://www.anvilstudio.com/, accessed 22/02/2008.

9 | Boys in a small rural school: Developing a culture of confidence and success

DANNY SPILLANE, Kentucky Public School, New South Wales

This chapter outlines how I developed and implemented whole-school teaching strategies aimed at improving the performance of boys by enabling students to access opportunities to succeed, building confidence and self-esteem and developing a positive school ethos. This was done using music as a primary focus and school theme. I was able to do this by drawing on my previous teaching experience as a teaching principal as well as accessing the support of a dedicated staff and an enthusiastic community.

Confidence is the hinge on the door to success. (Mary O'Hare Dumas)

When I took over the principalship of my previous school in June 2004, there were many issues facing staff, particularly concerns relating to student behaviour, school direction and academic achievement and, in general, problems relating to confidence and success. This was a particular problem with the boys in the school, who were often disruptive. These concerns were well justified, with suspensions occurring weekly, school planning lacking direction and basic academic skills data placing the school's male students in the lowest five schools of their region. These students seemed almost accustomed to, or accepting of, failure, and many had poor perceptions of themselves. They were at risk of continual school failure, and a major turn-around was required, as 'waiting for children to fail reduces self esteem and rarely sees the group catch up with age related peers' (Ainley & Fleming, 2000, p. 17).

The school had also been through a time of staffing upheaval, mainly in the area of school leadership, having four principals within a period of only 18 months. Without effective and stable leadership, it was difficult for sustained progress to be achieved, or for effective programs to reach their potential. This is supported by evidence suggesting that the principal plays a crucial role in a successful school (Raban & Essex, 2003). After consultation with staff and parent groups, a strategy was agreed upon and put into place. This strategy had a major focus on developing student confidence through the provision of opportunities for success. Through this, it was felt that many of the school's fundamental problems could be addressed, that boys would begin to achieve success more in line with their female peers and that a more positive school climate would be developed. Ownership and involvement by the staff, parents and the village community was deemed to be an integral factor in the success of the programs to be implemented. Recent research shows that children who have a strong sense of connection with their communities and feel safe and can trust those around them are more likely to achieve success at school (Ainsworth, 2002). Solomon, Battisch, Watson, Schaps et al. (2000) also found correlations between a sense of community and increased academic performance, positive social development and personal wellbeing.

Having had previous involvement in the implementation of similar programs that had achieved high levels of success and been accompanied by improved student academic results in both boys and girls, particularly when incorporating aspects of the performing arts, I felt confident that through achieving student success, developing confidence and encouraging a positive school culture, improvements in other key learning areas would follow.

Implementation

All of us do not have an equal talent, but all of us should have an equal opportunity to develop our talent. (John F. Kennedy)

I, too, believe that all students should have equal access to opportunity, including those in isolated areas. In 28 years of teaching, I have yet to see a program that addresses the above issue better than the one I am about to describe. Its aim was to provide a new focus for the school, based on musical performance. Creating their own set of marimbas and a range of other exotic instruments, students quickly developed into a quality performing group. The instruments were constructed using a range of basic materials and following designs created specifically for use in primary schools. Within days these students were performing for parents on school assemblies, and were soon entertaining local community groups such as the Country Women's Association, senior citizens and hospital groups, for which they received payment. The funds were deployed for the purpose of extending the program. They combined with the State Small Schools Marimba Ensemble, and performed at the Sydney Opera House Instrumental Festival less than a term after the program had begun. They eventually became one of the leading schools in this state group, performing at the Opera House again in 2006 and 2007, and at the Annual Schools Spectacular at the Sydney Entertainment Centre every year from 2004 to 2007. This event has recently been placed in the Guinness Book of Records as the World's Largest Variety Show.

Figure 9.1: Instruments made by the students, staff and parents of the school
– marimbas, wacky instruments and echocellos

The major strengths and achievements of this program include:

- The speed at which all students achieve success: most are playing basic pieces and able to join in within minutes.
- The whole–school involvement of the program; that is, all students from Years K to 6, take part, with boys equally involved.

- The low cost to the school, with each instrument being made for less than the cost of a day's casual teacher relief.
- All students and parents can be involved in the construction of the instruments, which are simple and fun to make.
- The high number of behavioural 'turn-arounds' from students who want to be involved and who are keen to experience the rewards of being involved.
- The opportunities the students have to fund their activities. Busking has proved very effective, with the group earning up to $500 per hour!
- The level of participation of boys as performers and their fathers in the construction phase (as well as that of girls and their mothers).
- The quality of the sound produced always delights those who hear them for the first time. I have had people peering under the instruments, looking for the CD player providing the 'backing' music who are then amazed to find that the entire sound is produced by the students.
- The relationship between two-handed playing and improved reading ability. This has been noted by many teachers involved in the program.
- The improvement of attitudes towards music by boys, who often perceive playing a musical instrument as a girl's habit, a belief particularly evident in more rural environments.
- The inter-school networking between students who are part of the state group, which I coordinate and conduct. This is of particular benefit in small communities, where peer groups are small.

I have been fortunate to have been involved in the implementation of this program into approximately 30 small schools across New South Wales, leading to over 300 students from isolated schools experiencing some amazing successes and performance opportunities. The networks established between teachers and students are extensive. All principals in the group are extremely positive about the effects of the program in their own schools. I have also seen the program implemented with equal success in two other schools at which I have been principal.

Apart from the above performances, the school's students also represented their school extremely successfully at several eisteddfods competing against much larger schools and in 2006, took part in the Federal Government's AARNET 3 (Australian Academic and Research Network) launch, which was beamed via satellite and the Internet across the globe. The increased self-esteem and confidence levels developed by this program alone turned the school into one in which success is enjoyed, anticipated and built upon.

The students were also given access to another amazing resource, in the form of the local community radio FM station, situated near the school. In 2004, I was made aware that the possibility of the students

Figure 9.2: Appearances at the Sydney Opera House and Entertainment Centre

running a weekly program was on offer, dependent on several factors. One of these was the undertaking by a member of staff to become proficient in the capacity of the program's supervisor, which involved becoming familiar with the station's operating procedure, including taking part in 'on air' responsibilities. The reason that this opportunity was not being accessed was that no staff member had been confident enough, or prepared to take on the role of supervisor. Seeing this as another wonderful opportunity to develop student confidence, promote the school and provide students with a unique opportunity, I took on the role.

The students prepared weekly news bulletins, organised song playlists, including requests, and presented their one-hour music show each Wednesday during the school term. The reading and writing element of the exercise was relevant to the students and had a clear purpose. These were prepared in the students' own time, with little need for teacher involvement. The program, 'Youth on Air' saw four students on air at a time, with every student given at least two term-long 'runs' during their time at the school. Some of the boys were particularly keen to highlight their own musical tastes on the show, which ranged from heavy metal to country and western.

The program was broadcast over several hundred square kilometres of northern New South Wales, with the parent body becoming avid listeners. The confidence built from the experience was rapid and clearly perceived each week. The self-direction the students continued to have of the program was also important, a point supported by Fullarton (1994, n.p.) who put forward that 'the confident students believed strongly in their ability to control their learning, and believed both that ability is necessary to do well and that they personally have the ability to succeed'.

Several other programs designed to increase confidence and provide opportunities for success were also implemented at the school. These included whole-school stage musicals, with input from all staff and parents. These were performed annually to sell-out audiences in the local hall and were eagerly awaited events by all members of the community. Students from an early age developed stage confidence and delighted in the 'kudos' of being involved on show night. The willingness for students to accept lead roles reinforced the success of the productions. Boys, who were in many instances reluctant to be involved in the first year of the events, soon became foremost in their willingness to take on larger, more demanding parts. This, in turn, provided effective role-modelling behaviour for their younger siblings and their peers.

Outcomes

The above programs all developed major levels of focus and self-esteem among the students at the school. Concentration and achievement levels have markedly improved, with basic skills test results above state norms in 90 per cent of cases in 2005 and 2006.

As evidenced by provided data:

- The growth in literacy and numeracy among Year 3 students (80 per cent boys) from my arrival at the school ranged between 12 and 14 points, which was over double the state norm (see appendices 9.1 and 9.2).
- Year 3 (75 per cent boys) results were also markedly improved, with 2006 results up to triple recent school averages (see appendices 9.3 and 9.4).
- By 2006, 100 per cent of students tested, using external data, had achieved national benchmarks in literacy and numeracy (see appendices 9.5 and 9.6).
- A reduced incidence of school suspensions from the high rates before the program's implementation to zero after its first year.
- Greater staff retention, improved school stability and parent/community satisfaction.

These trends continued until the time of writing.

In 2007, the school was nominated as a finalist in the state competition for the ABC Classic FM Flame Award. These awards recognise quality music programs, and in 2007 focused on the most 'innovative, impactful and inclusive' music program in primary schools. Due to the achievements of the students and the overall effectiveness of the school's programs, the school was successful in winning the New South Wales State Award and named the Classic FM Flame School for 2007.

> What guides us is children's response, their joy in learning to dance, to sing, to live together. (Yehudi Menuhin)

Another measure of the success of the strategies employed was the reactions of the students themselves. They became highly motivated and were eager to be involved, learn new pieces, improve their playing or singing skills, develop totally new skills or apply them in other areas of their school work. The benefits of high levels of motivation among students were highlighted by Skinner and Belmont (1993), who stated that:

> ... highly motivated students are enthusiastic, interested, involved and curious. These students try hard and persist, and they actively cope with challenges and setbacks. These are the students who are most likely to stay in school longer, learn more, feel better about themselves and continue their education past secondary school.

The expectation that whenever the students present an item of work or a presentation it is of high quality, has resulted in this actually being far more often the case than not. Aristotle said that 'We are what we repeatedly do. Excellence then is not an act, but a habit', and this is certainly the case. Students are only too aware when they are involved in something that they are not happy with quality wise, and will perform accordingly, displaying classic self-fulfilling prophecies. I have witnessed this time and time again when competing against other groups at eisteddfods and creative arts festivals, where boys, in particular, take to the stage with an air of defeat about them before a note has been played.

The major focus on the development of self, through increased alternative learning opportunities, raised confidence and self-esteem levels and the shared experiences of success, have been the foundation on which the school's current strengths have been built. These have turned around the performances of all students, especially boys, and will provide its direction in the coming years.

I am also extremely passionate in the beliefs highlighted throughout this chapter, and felt that this enthusiasm spread throughout the school community during my principalship there. This is summed up in the following quote, from one who was certainly passionate about learning:

> *I believe that education is all about being excited about something. Seeing passion and enthusiasm helps push an educational message. (Steve Irwin)*

References

Ainley, J. & Fleming, M. (2000). *Learning to Read in the Early Primary Years*. Melbourne: ACER Press.

Ainsworth, J.W. (2002). Why Does it Take a Village? The mediation of neighbourhood effects on educational achievement, *Social Forces*, *81*, pp. 117–52.

Fullarton, S. (1994). Motivation in Mathematics: Perceived control, engagement and achievement in the classroom, paper presented at Australian Association for Research in Education, Newcastle, 4 December.

Raban, B. & Essex, G. (2003). The Literacy Block in Primary School Classrooms, in R. Fisher, G. Brooks & M. Lewis (eds), *Raising Standards in Literacy*, pp. 216–30, London: Routledge.

Skinner, E.A. & Belmont, M.J. (1993). Motivation in the Classroom: Reciprocal effects of teacher behaviour and student engagement across the school year, *Journal of Educational Psychology, 85* (4), pp. 571–81.

Solomon, D., Battisch, V., Watson, M., Schaps, E. & Lewis, C. (2000). A Six-district Study of Educational Change: Direct and mediated effects on child development, *Social Psychology of Education, 4*, pp. 3–15.

Appendices

Appendix 9.1

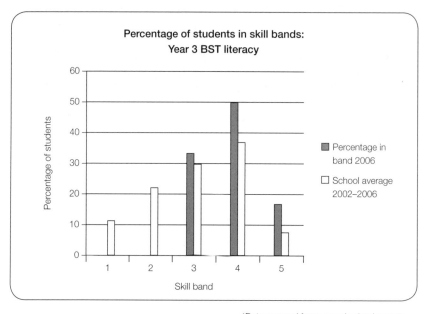

*Data sourced from annual school reports.

Appendix 9.2

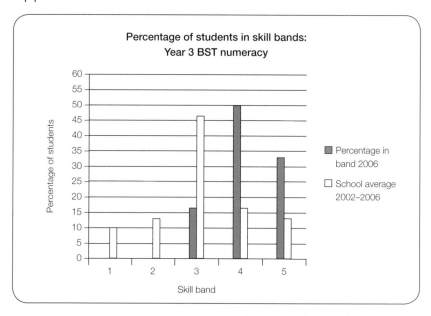

*Data sourced from annual school reports.

Appendix 9.3

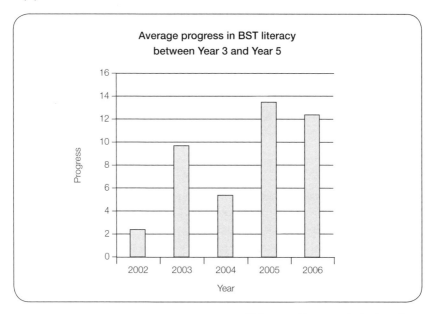

*Data sourced from annual school reports.

Appendix 9.4

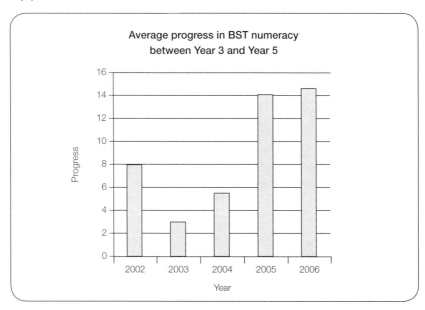

*Data sourced from annual school reports.

Appendix 9.5

Percentage of Year 5 students meeting national benchmarks				
	2005		2006	
	School	National	School	National
Reading	100	87.5 ± 1.8	100	88.4 ± 1.6
Writing	83	93.3 ± 1.3	100	93.8 ± 1.3
Numeracy	100	90.8 ± 1.3	100	90.3 ± 1.3

Source: National benchmarks sourced from: MCEETYA. (2005). *National Report on Schooling in Australia, Preliminary Paper. National Benchmark Results, Reading, Writing and Numeracy, Years 3, 5 and 7;* MCEETYA. (2006). *National Report on Schooling in Australia, Preliminary Paper. National Benchmark Results, Reading, Writing and Numeracy, Years 3, 5 and 7.*

Appendix 9.6

Percentage of Year 3 students meeting national benchmarks				
	2005		2006	
	School	National	School	National
Reading	83	92.7 ± 1.6	100	93.0 ± 1.7
Writing	100	92.8 ± 1.6	100	93.9 ± 1.3
Numeracy	100	94.1 ± 1.1	100	93.0 ± 1.4

Source: National benchmarks sourced from: MCEETYA. (2005). *National Report on Schooling in Australia, Preliminary Paper. National Benchmark Results, Reading, Writing and Numeracy, Years 3, 5 and 7;* MCEETYA. (2006). *National Report on Schooling in Australia, Preliminary Paper. National Benchmark Results, Reading, Writing and Numeracy, Years 3, 5 and 7.*

10 | Singing throughout life at Melbourne High School

CURTIS BAYLISS, ANNE LIERSE and JEREMY LUDOWYKE,
Melbourne High School, Victoria

I would teach children music, physics and philosophy;
but more importantly music; for in the patterns of music
and all the arts, are the keys to learning. (Plato)

Few matters have preoccupied the Australian educational community over the past two decades as consistently as concerns about the academic and social outcomes of young men. Many schools have struggled to engender a pro-learning, socially positive climate among their young men, especially when prevailing notions of masculinity and peer-group culture are antithetical to these good intentions.

As the foreword to the 2002 parliamentary inquiry into boys' education notes, '[b]oys are not achieving as well as they could, their years of schooling are less enjoyable and less rewarding and they face greater risk of unemployment, under-fulfilment and social problems in their post-school years' (Commonwealth of Australia, 2002, p. vii). This inquiry found that, across OECD countries, boys were increasingly disengaged from schooling, were more inclined than girls to misbehave and be truant, and that their post-school social and wellbeing outcomes were similarly in decline. Without any doubt, the main villain of this malaise is the repressive straitjacket of hegemonic notions of Australian masculinity. The taciturn and reserved nature of the traditional 'Aussie bloke' may have delivered dividends in past times; however, its prevailing strictures of emotional inexpressiveness and denial of feeling and interdependence have increasingly proved to be a recipe for personal and relational isolation and despair (McLean, 1995; Martino, 1995; Harrison, 2001a).[1]

These are extremely complex matters that require considered and complex responses, but research has shown that engagement in the arts can have a positive impact (Catterall & Waldorf, 1999). Melbourne High School in Victoria is a living example of this. This select-entry, Years 9–12 state school caters for nearly 1400 boys from an expansive array of cultural and socio-economic backgrounds. It is unique in being the only remaining government boys' school, as well as being, in conjunction with its sister school, the oldest secondary school in the state. Each year, its students attain the most outstanding academic results in the state, and it has contributed the largest university entry cohort of any school for over 100 years. Given its unsurpassed academic record, it comes as a surprise to many prospective students and their families that massed singing remains a central and compulsory component of the school's program, right through to the final week of Year 12. The school's educational philosophy is rooted in the liberal–humanist tradition of the 'well-rounded' individual. As it is often explained to the boys, this is an education of 'mind, body and spirit'. Nowhere in the school is this gestalt better exemplified than in the practice and experience of singing.

But in what sense does massed singing offer a panacea for the turbulent trials of masculinity? The social power of gender identity rests in its capacity to proscribe access to the full range of human traits to those considered to be culturally appropriate to your gender, at the cost of eschewing those that are not. This can condemn both men and women to a half-life and, in the case of men, to one marked by denial of emotional expression and interdependence, often in spite of their own best intentions and desires.

For young men, this constraint is heightened by a powerful and realistic fear of potential humiliation, rejection and reprisal from their peers if they transgress the appropriate gender boundaries. Massed singing is a potent subversion of the strictures of masculinity because it compels young men to collaboratively and publicly transgress these boundaries. Once you have convinced a bunch of young men that it is okay to stand alongside their peers and sing together, and to do so lustily, the barriers and restraints are set aside and, from that moment, anything is possible. We have borne witness to choirs of teenage boys performing soppy love ballads before an assembly of their peers, with accompanying hip rolls and shimmies, not to ridicule, but to applause and acclaim.

It is not just the cultural barriers that will be set aside. Once these young men have experienced the potential of a peer culture that is positive and affirming, both they and their teachers can recreate the same dynamics in the classroom and beyond. And the effects are life-long, as a graduate of a major private school decried: 'The trouble with Melbourne High School boys is that not only can't they stop talking about their school but if there are more than one of them talking to you, they suddenly start singing the School song' (Gregory, 2005, p. 568).

A massed singing program is a simple and cost-effective means of generating a strong collective sense of community, pride, respect, self-expression and group expression. In an era in which there are few rituals and ceremonies for young people, massed singing imparts a sense of cultural occasion and purpose. Few students have encountered any equivalent experience previously, yet no prerequisite expertise or talent is necessary, except for a willingness to participate and intelligently explore the music.

But will young men readily recognise and delight in these benefits? Recently, the principal visited each Year 12 class in the school imme-diately prior to their final exams. Each student was asked to nominate the features of the school program they found most helpful to their final preparation. The school's singing program was mentioned so often that he began to ask about it more directly. With the pressure of final exams looming large, these students affirmed that singing 'was bliss'. It not only provided a catharsis from mounting tension, but also a powerful sense of camaraderie and renewal of shared purpose. Remarkably, these same sentiments were very eloquently expressed by one Melbourne High student almost exactly 100 years earlier, in September 1907:

> *Our singing lessons are such that they rank amongst the most pleasant of all. They are at the same time invigorating and tranquillising. A 'tuneful tonic' without which our work would, at times, tend to the monotonous. The students seem to enter into the spirit of the songs and to enjoy the mental recreation they afford. (Vox Humana, 1907)*

The conceptual founder of the school and of state secondary education in Victoria, Frank Tate, described the principal educational benefit of singing as being its capacity to engender 'vital feelings of delight' (Tate, 1914). Over 100 years later, Melbourne High School students continue to affirm this axiom. Anyone who remains unconvinced that singing has the capacity to move cultural mountains is invited to attend any of the school's weekly assemblies and witness for themselves the power of song.

> *The soul of Melbourne High School is expressed through its singing. (Jeremy Ludowyke, Principal)*

The above quotation from the principal of Melbourne High School reflects the philosophical underpinning for the value placed on music in

Figure 10.1: Singing at Speech Night, Vodafone Arena, 2004

Source: Reproduced with permission of Melbourne High School.

the school. Singing is firmly entrenched in the ethos and traditions of Melbourne High School, and has been regarded as a valued activity for the students and staff since the school began in 1905.

The music program

The development and maintenance of the music program demands a high level of support from the school and, in particular, requires dedicated educational leadership from the principal. The music department has an exceptional team of four classroom music staff and 16 visiting specialist instrumental teachers, and is led by a director of music with a leading teacher appointment. A number of staff are actively involved in research, and regularly present workshops and seminars in the community. The 26 student ensembles, including a symphony orchestra of 90 players, a military band, the Stage Band and the two choirs – the Melbourne High School Singers and the Chorale – present in excess of 55 performances each year. The ensembles tour nationally and internationally, and participate in peak conferences, such as the International Society for Music Education. The school also combines with its sister school, The MacRobertson Girls' High School, for the annual musical theatre production, a jazz /improvisation concert and an annual concert.

Music curriculum

All Years 9 and 10 students have a timetabled, massed singing session each week. This session is in addition to the core classroom music program for Year 9 students and any of the six elective music subjects in Year 10, currently taken by more than 200 boys. The school also offers a comprehensive range of classroom, instrumental and ensemble subjects across Years 9 to 12, including a full range of Year 12 music studies. Approximately 600 students join one or more of the instrumental ensembles or choirs, and over 300 boys choose to learn an instrument or voice from one of the visiting specialist music teachers. The breadth of the program is reflected in the music department's vision statement:

* To have every student choose to be actively involved in the classroom and instrumental music program from Years 9 to 12
* To provide an exemplary whole-school singing program, choral and ensemble program at an international standard
* To provide leadership in Australia for the music education of boys.

Why such an emphasis on music in a highly academic school?

According to Stevens (2004), only 23 per cent of government schools offered access to a music education, in contrast to 80 per cent of independent schools. This was despite research that increasingly justifies music as an essential component in the education of the child. Melbourne High School's commitment to music education is informed by research demonstrating that a well-taught, sequential music education program will result in accelerated development in students' non-musical competencies. In addition, music can motivate students' interest in learning, develop their self-confidence, self-discipline and, most importantly, enrich their lives.

There is empirical evidence supporting the non-musical benefits of a competently delivered music education. A longitudinal study in the United States of 23,000 students, collected by seven national research teams, is documented in *Champions of Change* (Catterall & Waldorf, 1999). Its major findings were that music and the arts provide young people with authentic learning experiences that engage their minds, hearts and bodies, and that the learning experiences are real and meaningful. It also found that the arts engage multiple skills and abilities, and that music learning nurtures the integrated development of cognitive, affective, creative, motor, social and personal competencies. As well as transforming the environment for learning, it provides new challenges for those students already considered successful. The arts also connect learning experiences to the world of real work (pp. ix–x).

One of these studies looked at involvement in the arts and academic success. Findings showed that students who played an instrument and were involved in ensembles achieved higher levels of mathematical proficiency by Year 12, and students who maintained instrumental music involvement through to Year 12 continued to demonstrate improved academic results. An example from the study showed that the probability that high socio-economic status students with high involvement in playing in band or orchestra would score the highest level in mathematics was 140 per cent higher than the average for all children (Catterall & Waldorf, 1999). Another study found that young people in 'high-arts' groups performed better than those in 'low-arts' groups, measured on creativity, fluency, originality, elaboration and resistance to closure, and that 'arts intensive groups were strong in their abilities to express thoughts and ideas, exercise their imaginations and take risks in learning' (Burton, Horowitz & Abeles, 1999, p. 36).

There are therapeutic benefits of engaging with music. Music has been found to be one of the greatest antidotes for depression (Hanser, 1990). Anxiety, loneliness and depression are diminished – three factors that are critical in coping with stress and in helping the control of aggression (White, 1985; Moore & Schultz, 1983). Brain research has also revealed positive benefits of playing music. Work carried out in the area of intelligence quotient (IQ) showed that the IQ of students having keyboard or voice lessons increased from their pre-lesson score more than students with no lessons (Schellenberg, 2004). Rauscher, Shaw, Levine, Wright et al. (1997) also found that playing music builds or modifies neural pathways related to spatial reasoning tasks that are crucial to high brain functions. Most importantly, there is empirical evidence supporting claims of the power of music to bring joy and beauty into people's lives, to transform the human experience, exalt the human spirit and induce multiple physiological and emotional responses (Sloboda, 1991). We know that music is not an adornment of life but a basic manifestation of being human. It is essential to the development of the whole person and the soul of a nation. It is, therefore, essential learning for the 21st century.

The education of boys:
Aesthetic and emotional development

Research on the separation of boys and girls for music classes for physiological and behavioural reasons has shown results of enhanced learning, improved attitudes and a de-stereotyping of the music classroom. A number of empirical studies have highlighted problems emerging from sex-stereotyped musical behaviours. Studies by Abeles and Porter (1978), and Delzell and Leppla (1992) found a masculine–feminine continuum of instrument choice. Singing was perceived to be feminine in studies by Bartle (1968), Harrison (2001b) and Hanley (1998). All found that most choir members in co-educational schools were girls, and that any boys who sang were considered feminine by implication. Green (1993, pp. 219–53) argues that boys and girls tend to restrict themselves to certain musical activities, for fear of intruding into the other sex's 'territory'. On the other hand, Harrison suggests that in single-sex boys' schools, boys did sing in choirs and listed a number of boys' school in Australia, including Melbourne High School, which had a high level of participation in solo, community and choral singing (Harrison, 2001b).

Willis (1999) alerts us to the need to ensure that our teaching in the arts and music encourages a stimulation of the senses. He argues that we need to be reaching into the souls of boys through musical activities that allow for powerful sensory expression, rather than giving classes lacking practical work and with closed-end outcomes.

As a former principal of Melbourne High School (1999 to 2005), Willis (2005) also asserts that the ability of music to develop children's aesthetic sensibility and cognitive meaning are perhaps the two most powerful arguments for music education. Music is a haven in which *all* children can express their feelings. Creating an environment in which emotional sensitivity can be nurtured and supported is important to all children, but very important for boys, many of whom have learned not to openly show their emotions and feelings. To deny or bury feelings will result in their intellects growing while their emotional development remains stunted. This developmental delay is as true for gifted students, who may have heightened intensity of emotions and feelings, as for less able students, who are learning how to deal with their emotions. Music and the arts provide new challenges for all students, including those already considered successful.

Music can be magic. It calls for and calls forth all human virtues: imagination, discipline, teamwork, determination. It enriches and inspires. (UK Crown, 2006)

Massed singing

Singing that energises the body and vitalises the spirit is a deeply rewarding experience (Bunch & Vaughn, 2004). Singing individually or en masse can provide access to experiences of musical beauty. It allows an emotional, aural and language contact with historical eras and cultures that are otherwise difficult to make personal. Singing is egalitarian music-making that links students in each year level and as a whole entity in cooperative expression.

Melbourne High School has a long-standing pride in the energetic spirit and excellence of massed singing and of elective vocal singing. A massed-singing program is a simple, direct and cost-effective means for generating whole-school involvement and unity. Singing is seen as a 'Melbourne High School way' of self-expression and group expression. It is interesting to see the reaction of visitors and 'outsiders' to the volume and commitment displayed by Melbourne High students in full vocal flight. Vocal activity helps our school's cultural solidarity and self-pride. At Melbourne High there is no audition, and no prior experience (or 'talent') is necessary. The willingness to participate and intelligently explore the music are the attributes required.

In this day and age, in which students have few rituals and ceremonies, at this secular school we have found that our collective singing contributes a sense of occasion and can help to build varieties of humour or levels of *gravitas* in ceremonies. Group singing is the first team-building experience requested of new Year 9 students. Few students, new to any school, will have been expected to do something of this nature together. It is notable that many senior teachers come to the singing sessions to observe various year levels' approach and manner towards massed singing. They see this as a likely indicator of student participation and attitude to group work in general.

Massed singing would seem to have been a common practice in schools in the 19th century. The *Colony of Victoria Education Act of 1872* lists 'Singing' as a recommended subject that should receive one period of instruction per week in the primary sector (Gregory, 2005, p. 3). Singing was provided to the 49 girls and 79 boys who began segregated classes at the precursor to Melbourne High School, The National Model School, in September 1854. Each school administration since has supported class-time singing. After World War II, and again during the more liberal 1970s (eras during which other schools appear to have dismissed the activity), massed singing at Melbourne High was further consolidated and extended by musically aware principals and supported by determined music teachers.

History or not

At Melbourne High School every student sings. At first it is very tentative, but eventually most boys make more than a token effort. By Year 12, the enthusiastic involvement, expertise and sheer volume of the singing are astonishing. Most boys eventually take the risk of letting go of their fears and begin to contribute their energy wholeheartedly into learning to make controlled beautiful singing. (Cropley, 2005)

Visitors may say 'no wonder your school sings … you've been part of a tradition for 100 years!' However, few students are aware of the historical lineage behind their weekly massed-singing activity. Any traditions, however, can be quickly established or destroyed. As former Assistant Director of Music Roland Cropley (1996–2004) writes: 'the issue of tradition, whilst it has value, is not the reason that anything survives in the vigorous competition for space in the school's curriculum' (Cropley, 2005, p. 175).

Delivering our massed-singing program

While many of our students may already play a musical instrument with some proficiency, we seek to strongly encourage *all* our students to experience music-making by singing in the weekly massed-singing sessions. Participation is an 'expectation' rather than deliberately touted by staff as 'compulsory'. For students not yet learning an instrument, these weekly sessions introduce students to the fundamentals of vocal work, encourage them to apply basic music performance etiquette and teach some solfege and sight reading. Our graduating Year 12 students are expected to be able to read music (or at least follow melodic contours and rhythms), sing simple parts in an ensemble and feel comfortable performing in public. Singing, even at this level, does have relevance to aesthetic education.

Massed-singing objectives

General aims of year-level singing:

- Participation and community
- Limited but valuable music-making for non-musical students
- Compels students to take on the role of 'performers/presenters'
- Exposure to diverse vocal–choral literature and other languages.

Specific musical aims of year-level singing:

- To build confident, healthy vocal expression
- To stabilise and assist range, tone quality and dynamic controls

- To develop contour-based notation reading
- To instil rhythmic accuracy
- To heighten pitch accuracy
- To extend abilities to retain assigned simple harmony parts.

During the past decade, our weekly sessions have focused most on varying the dynamic range, and on keeping the singing 'sustained'; that is, remaining physically and tonally activated during the singing of long notes, across long phrases and from one sustained phrase to another. These elements are more frequently mentioned in our work than pitch-matching or just 'getting the right note'. We tread the line carefully between energetic, loud, massed 'bel canto' singing and 'yelling *can belto*'. Almost every weekly session includes some brief exercises to enhance the boys' breathing and their awareness of the vocal instrument. We tweak tuning or inner-hearing, cultivate presentation skills and learn to memorise the songs, which are shared with the staff and the school community each term.

The song choices are chosen to appeal to our students' sense of curiosity. They are given challenging material that, when well performed, gives a strong sense of achievement. Repertoire is chosen to give students enjoyment while developing the technical singing abilities and improving general musical understanding.

Generally, new students begin by learning the school song, 'Honour the Work'; they then tackle traditional folk and simpler pop songs before experiencing part-singing though the singing of rounds. Gradually, they are introduced to the more complex intervals and harmonies of jazz, musical theatre and contemporary music. Eventually, choruses by Beethoven, Verdi, Wagner and Orff are performed. A favourite with the students has been Puccini's 'Nessun Dorma'. Where possible, Australian compositions (such as those by Stephen Leek, Neil Finn, Paul Kelly and former student Colin Brumby) are promoted. We also 'mine the archives' for effective traditional or school-related songs, which have included Harrow School's sport song, 'Forty Years On' and Frederic Earp's 1914 Melbourne High School song, 'Best School of All'.

Songs are an excellent resource for providing glimpses of Australian culture and identity to a school whose population is so ethnically varied. In addition to pieces in French, German, Italian and Latin, the Speech Night selections have included works of the significant ethnic groups in the school. The Melbourne High Chorale has also sung Sonny Chua's arrangements in Hindi, Mandarin, Hokkien, Spanish and Maori.

As a secular institution attempting to welcome all creeds, songs are consciously selected to reflect worthy values. We require a cultural and religious sensitivity, which, while not precluding the singing of Christian hymns (a staple of former times) leads us to seek out various 'inspirational songs' and pieces with general 'spiritual' value. We also openly invite students to make repertoire suggestions.

A recipe for massed singing

Ingredients

- One large hall, filled with school boys, music teachers and other staff
- One pianoforte with player
- A microphone and public address system
- A projection screen
- Music score, or words alone via an overhead projector (or nowadays projections from a computer via data projector)

Figure 10.2: Year 9 students demonstrating their skills in 'choralography'

Method

We know that hard-bitten, sceptical teenagers have firm group tastes and won't be condescended to by well-intentioned teachers, but also that once aroused, their enthusiasm can be powerful. (Deveson, 1999)

Working with such a large group, either 350 or 700 boys at each session (1380 in dress rehearsals), there is a constant need to be looking to head off potential misunderstandings, or opportunities for pupil subversion. Conducting a year-level chorus or massed-singing session requires a few special teaching strategies:

- Keep verbal directions simple and positive.
- Maintain the rehearsal pace ... allow breaks/respites, then clearly indicate the return to a physical 'singing posture'.
- State the aim of any repetitions of material when resuming singing.
- Radiate a sense of humour, energy and positive goodwill.
- Make sure all visual presentations are clear and visible to all.
- Invite students to make repertoire suggestions.
- Select repertoire that engages and educates, and possibly also entertains.
- Provide songs in the right key for the particular group.
- Use good translations of foreign-language songs.
- Model good enunciation and know the correct pronunciation of foreign-language texts.
- Give an historical/cultural context for all works and settings.
- Be able to demonstrate the required musical style accurately, such as swing, dotted rhythms etc.
- Stir students' imagination and emotions with appropriate repertoire, and teach passionately.
- Use team teaching techniques and a variety of conductors where possible.

Despite the very good self-discipline of our students, having a number of general supervising teachers in the rehearsal space is important. Their presence reinforces the focus, participation and discipline of the students, and provides a sense of whole-school community and purpose.

Any process needs to be realistic, manageable and free of any preciousness. Humour and imagination are our greatest allies! Boys in drama classes generally produce a freer vocalisation and a greater variety of volume than those in music classes, because drama students work in an environment in which imagination and emotional risk taking are encouraged.

Ultimately, student cooperation, some good repertoire, a surety of purpose and a teacher with personality for connecting with a large body of students are required for such massed singing to succeed. It also relies very heavily on the quality of the accompanist(s), and the support of the principal and the general staff.

With absolutely no desire to simply replicate any private schools, past or present, it is useful to reflect on the sentiments expressed in a lecture by a school music director, Clement Spurling of Oundle School,

England in 1928. Such sentiments would be warmly endorsed by today's Melbourne High music staff:

> *Wholehearted singing is expected from every boy and, if necessary, insisted upon. Probably a small percentage of boys can never hope to get near a tune, but inability to sing is never admitted for one moment. The wrong notes of the few do not matter among the right ones of so large a number ... If the parts do not balance I do not mind ... get every boy to take part in the singing ... I will try to make the performance as good as possible. I am not preparing a performance of music I want the whole world to hear, I am preparing it because I want every boy to learn the music. (Spurling, 1928, n.p.)*

Spurling and Headmaster Sanderson of Oundle School in Northampton-shire, United Kingdom, became famous for their school's spirited annual performances of oratorios, such as Handel's Messiah and Bach's B minor Mass by the whole school of 580 boys.

A performance deadline is vital. At Melbourne High School, the year-level choruses perform at end-of-term Singing Assemblies. The Year 10 students (approximately 360 boys) form half of the choir for the annual Legacy Anzac Schools' Service at Melbourne's Shrine of Remembrance in April. Years 9 and 10 students combine with Years 11 and 12 students in term one at the House Choral Competition and in term four for Speech Night.

Music Assemblies at the end of each term, before an audience of staff and guests, provide performance opportunities for the pieces mastered in the weekly sessions. In the Music Assembly marking the end of term three, a work being considered for next term's Speech Night is usually test-driven. These 'in-house' performances also help to prepare students for the disciplines and stamina needed for the public Speech Night performance.

The House Instrumental and Choral competition, for which every boy sings for his house, establishes a 'singing energy' in the school at the beginning of each year. This exciting and competitive, day-long, whole-school singing event in the first term, co-administered with the director of sport, shows the talents of each of the school's four houses (Como, Forrest, Waterloo, Yarra) in producing massed singing, chamber choir and instrumental items. Lynn Richardson, then-director of The Australian Girl's Choir, having just adjudicated the 2004 competition, commented in amazement: 'It was a celebration of striving forward towards a goal that, while it was competitive, wasn't like a sport, but instead was all to do with the beauty of music making'.

Additional educational outcomes of this competition are the work-shop training and practical experience given to teams of young choral and instrumental conductors, the skilling of the accompanists, and the notated and tested choral arrangements created by the students.

Speech night

Daniel May, an Australian organisational analyst, has explored a number of corporations and organisations in Europe and Australia for their 'culture building' process. One of May's sites for observation was Melbourne High School at its annual Speech Night:

> The event is a powerful cultural tool in the life of the School. It is held in the city's large Town Hall (now in an 8000 seat stadium), comprising academic awards, a comprehensive music program, and a speech delivered by a famous past student of the School. Throughout the evening, each part of the program reinforces the School's metaphor of itself as 'crème de la crème'. The high point of the evening is the massed singing by the 1200 (now 1370) students who attend the School, who have been practising for many weeks prior to the evening. The first year student is typically shaped in a profound way by this evening: he has participated in a ritual of rehearsal and execution of an event that every boy in the school has experienced, one that points to many other aspects of the School's culture (e.g. music, academic excellence, involvement in the community). After that he knows he is part of a distinctive group and culture. (May, 2001, p. 11)

The success of singing at these events is only possible because of our students' willingness to cooperate, to sing, and to sing out loud. These intelligent young men give each other 'permission', to sing spiritedly and with confidence.

The experience of performing in public influences a reasonably large proportion of students to better appreciate other performers. Weekly massed-singing sessions help to generate a school-wide acceptance and culture of singing.

Singing throughout life!

Melbourne High students take this vocal life into the wider community, to their tertiary studies and beyond. A surprisingly high number of our graduates participate in professional, amateur and community music making. Does it also suggest a reason so many of our students subsequently feel comfortable in the 'theatrical' professions of university, legal and political life? The list of famous old-boy composers, musicians and singers (in all genres) is impressive, perhaps the more so because the basis of selection for entry to the school has remained academic (never

Figure 10.3: Speech Night 2006, Vodafone Arena

on musical ability). Melbourne High School has never been regarded as a specialist 'music school'.

Elective singing

It is probable that the elective vocal and choral activities are as well supported as they are because the weekly massed-singing sessions help to generate a school-wide acceptance and culture of singing. Elective singing activities include: private and group voice lessons; participation in 'project choirs', such as the six-rehearsal Finale Choir for the Winter Concert; and the annual School Musical or 'Opera'. Boys may also join the un-auditioned group of about 70 students who sing as the Melbourne High School Chorale, or the Melbourne High Singers – an auditioned, close-harmony group of 21 singers with student accompanist. There is also the student-run Barbershop Society and a number of boy-bands. Some of the school's sports groups also sing together to raise money and to intimidate opponents!

In such an academically focused school, however, some students (or their parents) are unwilling to commit to involvement in regular ensembles, but rather choose to volunteer for a short-term 'project'. These projects include the annual music theatre production, labelled 'the Opera' (begun in 1961) and a few after-school and weekend rehearsals for the massed Winter Concert Finale choir. Both of these projects may also become more attractive to our boys because they are cooperative ventures with our sister school, the MacRoberston Girls' High School.

Some 35 students take voice lessons in their school hours with a voice teacher supplied by the Education Department. Many of these voice students have continued singing in the community well beyond their school days. Other students may choose to join with smaller ensembles with special interests and advanced singing abilities, focusing on deeper musical issues, such as the stylistic and aesthetic aspects of a musical piece.

Figure 10.4: Melbourne High School Chorale

Source: Reproduced with permission of Melbourne High School.

Melbourne High School Chorale can be regarded as the school's 'choir', being un-auditioned and open to all interested students. Sonny Chua (Director of the Melbourne High School Chorale 2002–7) created remarkable group energy during his time as director of the Chorale. This choir has done much to excite the public and other music educators to the possibilities of young men performing. Lately, the group's repertoire has been almost entirely arranged or composed by Chua himself, who frequently utilises the lower ranges of the bass and baritone voice in two and three parts. His works were carefully chosen to allow performance by an ensemble that fluctuated from 30 to 80 volunteers. His settings, with catchy flamboyant piano or instrumental accompaniments for performance by students, frequently explored Asian and European cultural references in many languages, and took advantage of his students' comic abilities.

Above all, the Chorale endeared itself to audiences by demonstrating a huge spirit of enjoyment and a passionate commitment to rich-toned singing, combined with the boys' own movement and dance sequences. Sonny Chua's choral arrangements are published and available for use by other groups of singers.

The Melbourne High School Singers are a smaller auditioned choir that tackle a wide variety of more complex part singing. It rarely dances.

Figure 10.5: Melbourne High School Singers, 1977

Source: Reproduced with permission of Melbourne High School.

Figure 10.6: Melbourne High School Singers, 2007

Source: Reproduced with permission of Melbourne High School.

Since its inception in 1977 by Peter Ross and Alwyn Mott, the Melbourne High School Singers has worked as a large close-harmony or swing choir of the more senior students. Repertoire is varied to suit the leanings and vocal qualities of each year's membership. The group regards itself as a 'large close-harmony group' rather than a 'choir', until it combines with other voices.

Since Curtis Bayliss became conductor (in 1999), members of the group have been selected from all four year levels. In the past few years it has been deliberately limited to 21 members. The group regularly combines with one of the school's large swing bands, the MHS Stage Band.

At the audition, the priorities are:

- Sight-reading ability
- Range and voice colour
- Intonation, recall-echo and part-singing ability.

Each singer is regarded as a responsible soloist and must be able to hold a part against other harmonies. Ideally, the group is made up of five balanced vocal quartets: a T.T.B.B. quartet from each year level, plus a vocal soloists' group and a piano accompanist who can sing. The auditionee's ability to arrange music for voices, his skills in languages and his proficiency on other musical instruments are taken into account. The group's style, tonal quality, repertoire and the assignment of parts alters from year to year (usually within the year as well), as it adjusts to the singers' changing voices. A priority in the past five years has been to include student compositions in the choir's repertoire and to perform the students' own arrangements.

The experience of singing in these elective vocal-choral ensembles leaves students with a wide variety of attitudes and skill levels. Following their secondary schooling, many of these students see music making as just another facet in their accomplishments and experience, but will not sing again. It is likely that they are at least a little more appreciative of the skills of performing and more vocally confident than they might otherwise have been. Other students leave the school eager to participate in tertiary or community music making. As would be expected, a small proportion of these students confidently apply for vocal scholarships to university, national youth and honour choirs, and places in music courses.

Melbourne High School succeeds in creating a high-scoring academic community of confident and articulate young men. It is all the more remarkable that at Melbourne High School, singing is so appreciated for promoting school pride and cooperative spirit in good measures of equity and enjoyment. Beautiful music is made but not at the expense of inclusion of as many students as possible. Singing as a whole-school activity strives for unity and enjoyable competition to co-exist.

The music staff and principal are keenly aware that real educational and institutional benefits must be gained to justify the inclusion of massed singing in the demanding curriculum. Staff and some old-boys are conscious that a change of personnel might all too quickly and easily put an end to this long tradition of whole-school singing. The rich offering of elective singing and instrumental tuition, and the varied ensemble options, including a high-standard school musical, are also remarkable in this school, which does not offer music scholarships nor is a designated 'music school'. Participation as performers / audience and the concepts imparted in the classroom study of music affect our students beyond their school days and do eventually impact on the greater Melbourne community. These intelligent young men venture into the world as more discerning music consumers, most generally confident to raise their voice, and at best ready to become even more skilled and sharing performers, composers, conductors and educators. Melbourne High School has helped provide many of the male voices in the musical life of this nation.

Endnote

1   See also Chapter 1 for a summary of this point.

References

Abeles, H.F. & Porter, S.Y. (1978). The Sex Stereotyping of Musical Instruments, *Journal of Research in Music Education, 26,* pp. 65-75.

Bartle, G. (1968*). Music in Australian Schools,* Australian Council of Music Education, Melbourne: Wilke & Company.

Bunch, M. & Vaughn, C. (2004). *The Singing Book*, New York: W.W. Norton.

Burton, J., Horowitz, R. & Abeles, H. (1999). Learning In and Through the Arts, In E. Fiske (ed.), *Champions of Change: The impact of the arts on learning,* pp. 35–46, Washington, DC: The Arts Partnership and the President's Committee of the Arts and Humanities.

Catterall, J.S. & Waldorf, L. (1999). Chicago Arts Partnerships in Education, Executive Summary evaluation, in E. Fiske (ed.), *Champions of Change: The impact of the arts on learning,* pp. viii–x, Washington, DC: The Arts Partnership and the President's Committee for the Arts and Humanities.

Commonwealth of Australia (2002). *Boys Getting It Right: Report on the inquiry into the education of boys*, Canberra: Commonwealth of Australia.

Cropley, R. (2005). Rituals, Assemblies and Singing, in J. Prideaux (ed.), *More Than Just Marks*, pp. 174–5, Melbourne: Pennon Publishing.

Delzell, J. & Leppla, D.A. (1992). Gender Association of Musical Instruments, *Journal of Research in Music Education, 40*(2), pp. 93–103.

Deveson, T. (1999). The Judges' Reports; Primary and secondary school-book award for music; TES competition, *The Times Educational Supplement*, www.tes.co.uk/section/story/?section= Archive&sub_section=Friday&story_id=313279&Type=0, accessed 13/02/2008.

Green, L. (1993). Music Gender in Education: A report on some exploratory research, *British Journal of Music Education, 10*, pp. 219–53.

Gregory, A. (2005). *Strong Like Its Pillars*, Melbourne: Langley, Courtis, Thompson Library Trust of Melbourne High School.

Hanley, B. (1998). Gender in Secondary School Music Education in British Columbia, *British Journal of Education, 15*(1), pp. 51–69.

Hanser, S.B. (1990). A Music Strategy for Depressed Older Adults in the Community, *Journal of Applied Gerontology, 9*(3), pp. 283–98.

Harrison, S.D. (2001a). Why Boys Limit Musical Choices: An initial report on some exploratory research into issues of participation by boys in musical activities, paper presented at Australian Education Assembly, Melbourne.

Harrison, S.D. (2001b). Real Men Don't Sing, *Australian Voice, 11*, pp. 31–6.

Martino, W. (1995). Gendered Learning Practices: Exploring the costs of hegemonic masculinity for girls and boys in schools, *Gender Equity: A framework for Australian schools* (pp. 122–44). Canberra: MCEETYA.

May, D.C. (2001). *Building the Cultural Artifacts of the Organization*, http://64.233.179.104/scholar?hl=en&lr=&q=cache:1ZJPy61t9 KQJ:www.thedanielmay.com/publications/cultural_artifacts_05. pdf+%22daniel+may%22+%22melbourne+high+school%22, accessed 22/03/2008.

McLean, C. (1995). The Costs of Masculinity: Placing men's pain in the context of male power, *Gender Equity: A framework for Australian schools* (pp. 85–8), Canberra: MCEETYA.

Moore, D. & Schultz, N.R. (1983). Loneliness at Adolescence: Correlates, attributions, and coping, *Journal of Youth and Adolescence, 12*, pp. 95–100.

Rauscher, F., Shaw, G., Levine, L., Wright, E., Dennis,W. & Newcomb, R. (1997). Music Training Causes Long-term Enhancement of Preschool Children's Spatial–temporal Reasoning, *Neurological Research, 19*, pp. 2–8.

Schellenberg, E.G. (2004). Music Lessons Enhance IQ, *Psychological Science, 15*(8) , pp. 511–14.

Sloboda, J.A. (1991). Music Structure and Emotional Response: Some empirical findings, *Psychology of Music, 19*, pp. 110–20.

Spurling, C.M. (1928). Music in the Public Schools of Today, in *Proceedings of The Musical Association of England* (pp. 1–17), http://links.jstor. org/sici?sici=09588442(1927%2F1928)54%3C1%3AMIPSOT%3E2.0.CO%3B2-G, accessed 13/03/2008.

Stevens, R. (2004). *Trends in the Provision of School Music Education*, Music Council of Australia, www.mca.org.au/index.php.id.273, accessed 4/02/2007.

Tate, F. (1914). *The High School Song Book*, Melbourne: High School Teachers' Association Victoria.

UK Crown (2006). *The Music Manifesto*, www.musicmanifesto.co.uk/key-aims, accessed 6/10/2008.

Vox Humana (1907). Anonymous student, *Our School Magazine*, Melbourne: Melbourne High School, p. 12.

White, A. (1985). Meanings and Effects of Listening to Popular Music: Implications for counselling, *Journal of Counselling and Development*, *64*, pp. 65–9.

Willis, R. (1999). The Role of Sensory Education in the Education of Boys, paper presented at the Cross Arts Seminar, Melbourne.

Willis, R. (2005). Learning to Think With Your Heart, in J. Prideaux (ed.), *More Than Just Marks*, pp. 9–19, Melbourne: Pennon Publishing.

11 | The Birralee Blokes

PAUL HOLLEY, Voices of Birralee

The Birralee Blokes, ABC Australian Choir of the Year in 2006, are the definitive young male voice choir in Australia today, working to reshape the stereotype of the male chorister. This chapter tells their story – from a small beginning to an ensemble of 50 young men, five years later. Through my 'voice' as their musical director, we explore the aim of providing an opportunity for young men to express themselves through the unique and wonderful sound of male choral singing. The creation of a relaxing, rewarding and empowering environment forms the philosophical basis for this goal.

This chapter outlines the Blokes' journey, from its initial aim to its present fulfilment, and provides suggestions in the hope of encouraging others who work with young male ensembles. The strongest words come from the Blokes themselves, who explain their experience of singing and the highlights and benefits of being a part of this male ensemble.

The Birralee Blokes is a community ensemble for teenage boys and young men with changing and changed voices. The choir is based in Brisbane, and draws its membership from the wider south-east corner of Queensland. Rehearsals are held on Saturday afternoons during the school term, for 90 minutes. Performances occur regularly at a variety of civic and community events. The Blokes have toured twice internationally. In 2005, the group attended Piccfest, a children's choir festival in Eugene, Oregon, in the United States. In 2007, they represented Australia at the 3rd British International Male Voice Choral Festival in Cornwall, United Kingdom. They have also toured within Australia, and twice have been invited to perform at the Australian National Choral Association conference, Choralfest. The Blokes have recorded two albums, *Come to the Music* (2004, along with other Birralee ensembles) and *walls come tumblin' down* (June 2006). In 2006, they were named ABC Classic FM

Choir of the Year, as well as Youth Choir of the Year, and received the
Listener's Choice Award in the inaugural, national Choir of the Year
competition.

Getting started

The Birralee Blokes was formed in May 2003, to fill a gap in the choral
scene by providing a vehicle for young men to continue singing through
the various stages of their voice-change process, in a safe, all-male
environment. The Voices of Birralee organisation is a community based
children's choir that acts as an extension activity for students who want
to pursue their love of choral singing beyond their school experiences.
The organisation was founded in 1995 by Julie Christiansen OAM, based
in the western suburbs of Brisbane and known as the Westside Youth
Choir. Over the following five years, the choir grew in size and developed
a reputation as a fine children's choir. In addition to the signature choir,
there was a group for 5–8-year-olds, known as the Piccolos, and a Junior
Choir that fostered the development of young voices. Just before the
choir's first international tour to Vancouver, Canada in early 2001, the
choir changed its name to Brisbane Birralee Voices.

In 2002, Artistic Director Julie Christiansen attended an Australian
National Choral Association (ANCA) conference in Brisbane. The
importance of providing opportunities for both girls and boys of this
age group to work independently was a feature of this event. As part
of this festival, ANCA organised secondary honour choirs for teenage
girls and boys. The boys' choir saw approximately 20 boys come from
various parts of Brisbane to sing together and to work with international
and national conductors. This experience fuelled Julie Christiansen's
desire to provide an environment for boys whose love for singing had
been nurtured for many years during their childhood and whose self-
esteem and identity were inextricably linked with their ability to sing.
Discussions with other children's choir directors across Australia
reinforced the awareness of the psychological trauma that some young
male singers experience as their voice changes.

Until this point, boys at Birralee would, as trebles, sing for as long
as possible in order to preserve their sense of identity. As their 'once
reliable' voices became more and more unpredictable, they would eventually submit to the reality of their changing voice. Having observed this
difficult transition for a number of years, Julie commented:

> I could not ignore the responsibility I felt to provide a secure environment for
> these boys for whom singing had become an intrinsic part of who they were.

A dedicated, all male ensemble would give them the opportunity to retain their passion and continue singing through the physical and emotional instabilities of adolescence.

As a result of this growing concern, Birralee resolved to trial an ensemble for boys with changing/changed voices. Discussions followed about how to get the ensemble started and how to recruit young men to be part of this experiment. It was decided to incorporate the boys into a camp that was already to be held for the Birralee Voices treble choir in May 2003. A weekend camp meant that there was time for the guys to begin creating a sound that was rewarding and the chance to build some cohesion as a group. The presence of almost 70 young women at the camp may have been an additional drawcard for some participants.

As there were already a few boys in the treble ensemble whose voices were changing, they would be part of the new ensemble. There was still a need to invite others to become involved. The concept was advertised through flyers and conference presentations, in the hope that 15–20 boys would accept the opportunity to be involved.

The camp brought together 17 boys from Brisbane, Toowoomba and Hervey Bay, in addition to the 70 other young people who were members of the Birralee Voices choir. The choir met for the first time on the Friday night, and over the course of the weekend worked both on their own repertoire and some SATB (soprano, alto, tenor and bass) repertoire with the treble choir as well. The male singers of The Australian Voices, with conductor Stephen Leek, also came and worked with the boys. This swelled the number of singers and proved to be a very useful modelling process. It also allowed the guys to gain an insight into the amount of sound that a group could make, and also the richness of tone that is a defining quality of male voice singing.

The boys worked extremely well and, while they had varying degrees of choral background, many of them were good sight singers. This meant that we were able to commence working on vocal tone and ensemble skills immediately. The ensemble presented its first performance at the camp concert on the Sunday afternoon. The pride in the faces of the boys when they heard the cheers from the audience was very moving and, although the first performance was not musically impressive, there was certainly a buzz about this new ensemble. At the end of the camp the boys were asked to consider whether they would like to continue singing with the group on a Saturday afternoon for the rest of 2003. Fourteen of the boys decided it was worth the time, and the choir's future was assured.

Finding a name for the ensemble was not easy. We wanted to incorporate the word Birralee so that the choir was recognisable as part of the organisation. We also wanted to avoid the word 'choir', as it was felt this had too many negative connotations for the average Australian male (see Chapters 1 and 2 for a more in-depth discussion of this issue). The term 'blokes' was suggested, but at first was thought to be too 'ocker' and perhaps too casual, although it did have the advantage of sounding masculine. Other possibilities were the Lads of Birralee, the Birralee Guys and Birralee Boys. The boys expressed a preference for 'blokes', and when the decision was finally taken, they embraced it immediately: the Birralee Blokes was formed!

The next step was to build the size of the ensemble, and a recruitment strategy was implemented. It was felt that the best way to increase the numbers in the group was to increase their profile, and so we looked for opportunities for the group to perform. Several of the boys came from the same local high school, so we sang at one of their concerts, and we also entered the Blokes in the Brisbane Eisteddfod. The knock-on effect was that more boys heard about the ensemble and the size of the group steadily increased. One boy who competed against the Blokes in the eisteddfod was the only male singer in his school choir. He enjoyed the school choral experience and his teacher encouraged him and accommodated his voice within an otherwise treble choir. The appeal in joining the Blokes was that he felt his singing was less exposed and he was less threatened in an all-male ensemble. From a timid and very quiet singer, he developed into a confident choral singer and soloist with the group. As the director of the ensemble, the reward of observing the personal development of this young man over the ensuing years has been extraordinary.

The philosophy

To sing is to be. (Rainer Maria Rilke)

Singing with others has been a part of life for centuries, with communities joining together to sing and participate, not just in the music but the joy of sharing that music with others. The Birralee Blokes is one such community, where a group of young men enjoy singing together for the experience of creating and performing beautiful music, and for the fun that they have doing it. I firmly believe that choral singing is fun, and that as a conductor I should make the experience of music making as enjoyable as possible for all those who sing in my choir. If I am not enjoying myself then I cannot expect that the singers in my choir will enjoy themselves. Choral singing is as much about the journey that the choir takes together in learning a song as it is about the final product. While the central motivation in the ensemble is to perform well, at a high standard, the discoveries made during the journey are just as vital. In addition to the expected musical discoveries, the social, psychological and, at times, spiritual growth that occurs is of far greater import.

The aim of forming the Birralee Blokes was to keep young men singing when their voices changed. Based on anecdotal information and a growing amount of research literature (Harrison, 2001; Adler, 2002; Phillips, 2003), we knew that the creation of a safe setting was required. Clare Hall (see Chapter 2) also notes that singing in a group outside of school is advantageous. Birralee Blokes established a place outside of school where young men experiencing the voice change could do so in a safe, *relaxed, rewarding* and *empowering* environment.

A relaxing environment

Barham and Nelson (1991) write:

> Singing is personal. It requires that the boy take a chance. At stake is not only his personal self-esteem, but also his social identity. The choir, under the leadership of the teacher, must become a support group. You are instructing in how to 'live', not just how to survive. The boy who feels confident that he will be accepted will be willing to take a chance … sing!

For the teenager, boy or girl, creating a non-threatening environment that allows them to express themselves and find an identity for themselves is pivotal to their social development and could be a core reason for them seeking a choral ensemble experience (see Adler & Harrison, 2004). As a choral director I can be single-minded, highly disciplined and striving for perfection as I aim to make the best music possible. This can mean that we approach our common world from very different angles. The challenge is to get the balance between allowing for self-discovery and expression, creating a beautiful choral sound and meeting the demands the composer has asked of the ensemble.

In order to create a beautiful sound, the vocal tone needs to be free and clear. For the boy with a changing voice, or a recently changed voice, this can be difficult, as nature conspires against him in some ways as he goes through the physiological changes that occur during this process.[1] There will be times when the boy feels as though he has no idea what is going to come out of his mouth, let alone be able to control it. For the teenage boy this can be scary and a real challenge to his self-confidence. The advantage of the all-male choir for the teenage boy is that all of his fellow singers in the ensemble are either going through (or have gone through) the same experience and therefore have an understanding of the insecurities that can accompany this time of life. My experience is that it doesn't stop them from having a laugh at one another's occasional squeaks! The fear of risking their masculinity in front of girls is removed in the single-sex setting, and they are more likely to take risks with their voices. To achieve the goal of 'free singing', I believe there must be an allowance given for the boys to feel that they can go for it no matter what comes out, and to be able to experiment with their vocal sound. If this atmosphere can be fostered in rehearsal, then it is amazing what can be achieved by the young male singer. It is imperative that while the boys are experimenting and discovering their new vocal sound, clear guidance is given to help them create a free, well-produced and well-projected tone. In my experience, if the environment is relaxed and safe they will be willing to take the required risks with their singing and discover what they are capable of.

Another aspect to consider in creating the relaxed environment is not musical. Teenage boys are a unique breed: very different physically, emotionally and psychologically from their female counterparts. To work with young men requires an understanding of the changes that are occurring in their world and how this will impact on the way they deal with others. It is important also to note that the stages of development and journeys taken by each individual will be very different. With this background, I determined that in the Blokes I would let the boys be themselves and embrace their individuality. The practical applications of this decision have meant that rehearsals are not sedate, controlled or regimented, but instead loud, dynamic and spontaneous. That is not to say chaotic and unfocused, but freedom is given to them to be themselves instead of conforming to a set stereotype. If this approach is to work there needs to be respect shown by all, to all. For the conductor, this means that in addition to a thorough musical knowledge, they need to accept each boy for who they are and what they bring to the ensemble, and be able to see their potential for growth and encourage them to fulfil this potential. For each chorister this means increasing their musical knowledge, accepting each other's differences, accepting guidance from the conductor and being willing to compromise in order to reach the collective goal of the ensemble.

A rewarding environment

For the amateur singer, choral singing is a pastime, not a job. There is a hope that the experience will be an enjoyable one. Having fun is a key component but not the sole factor in the enjoyment. For the singer there is a desire to create a wonderful musical experience that is rewarding. The reward can take many forms, but it is pivotal to continuous improvement and enjoyment. For the Blokes, the rewards have come through audience accolades and success at competitions.

From early performances, audiences have responded positively to the Blokes. The rare sight of a group of teenage boys singing together has engaged and, indeed, excited many audiences of all ages. The novelty factor is high and, without even singing a note, the boys often feel that they have the audience with them. A colleague once noted that a young male voice choir could sing a C major chord and the audience would go wild. For continuing audience interest, the product on offer has to be engaging and entertaining. Similarly, the singers presenting the product need to be engaged by it. The selection of repertoire is therefore very important in this regard. There is such diversity in the choral repertoire available to choirs nowadays, with music from all parts of the world and from all periods of history available to discover. In selecting repertoire, there needs to be a balance between pieces that will be easily sung and those that present a challenge technically, musically and interpretatively. The conductor should always be on the look out for pieces that will provide a new experience for the singers. For the Blokes, after singing predominantly folk music and music theatre repertoire in our early stages, the technical and musical challenges of singing classical repertoire have become more rewarding. For example, the Blokes were recently able to perform *Salvation is Created* (Chesnokov) and *Du bist die Ruh* (Schubert). The reward came in their ability to sing the notes and words, and also in their capacity to change the sound to meet the demands of the music. An additional factor was in the audience's appreciation of the beautiful music created.

Much of the research into the psychology of gender, states that, among other stereotypes, men can be aggressive and competitive (Maccoby, 1966; Susman, Feagans & Ray, 1992; Beall & Sternberg, 1993). Aggression, according to Eagly and Steffen (1984) is determined by social norms, situational factors, attitudes and previous learning history. With a group of teenage boys in a rehearsal room, these traits are occasionally displayed as they interact with one another. To varying degrees, the competitive streak is one that is evident among the boys, and they sometimes feel the need to outdo one another. In order to maintain a relaxed and efficient environment, this is dealt with expeditiously, but the natural competitive edge can be beneficial when harnessed collectively.[2] With the announcement of our entry in the ABC Classic FM Choir of the Year competition, the sense of excitement was palpable. Once the Blokes were selected for the state final, the intensity of rehearsals increased as they focused in greater detail on the musical goals they were trying to achieve. This level of intensity grew exponentially as they prepared for the national final. The guys discovered a new level, well beyond the accuracy of the notes and the text: they realised that interpreting and conveying music involved so much more than they had previously understood. There is no doubt that the competition was the catalyst for this discovery. Beyond the excitement of winning the competition, the choir had their sound and performance style validated by the both the adjudicators and the Australian public through the Listener's Choice Award. The ongoing benefits have been appreciable:

- For individuals, there is an increased level of confidence gained from winning the competition.
- For the choir, there is a consistently higher level of musicality.
- For the broader community, there is an increase in the awareness and acceptance of singing for boys and young men singing in Australia.

As a result, singing as a rewarding experience is one that hopefully more young men will discover. As one of the Blokes said, 'singing is fun, pure and simple. It's our natural inclination to want to sing as men, regardless of what society says'. Anecdotally, music educators have noted that the Blokes have provided an authentic model of masculinity for young Australian males.

An empowering environment

So often in musical ensembles the director controls all aspects of the group. Members feel that they would be nothing without the conductor, and that the group would cease to function if that person were no longer able to carry out the role as director. This sole reliance on the director as guru is unhealthy and stifles the development of the people in the ensemble.[3] I strongly believe that my role as conductor is to empower the young men in my ensemble so that they improve their skills, increase their self-confidence and perhaps eventually take on leadership positions in choral music.

While motivating, directing and managing the choir is largely the domain of the conductor in the early stages, the ultimate goal is for the members of the ensemble to take ownership of the choir; in particular, ownership of the choir's sound and presentation of the music. This involves them taking the responsibility for making sure that their music is thoroughly known and that they present themselves and the music they are performing well. It can also mean the boys taking on other responsibilities in the choir. Peer leadership can be a very powerful tool but it can also cause division. Some choirs employ section leaders to control behaviour and lead musically, but this is not an approach used with the Blokes. Instead, each boy is encouraged to take responsibility for his behaviour and focus in a rehearsal. When there are sectionals to be done the boys are sent away to do the work in their voice parts and they are collectively responsible for learning their notes. As one Bloke said, 'If someone is not prepared, the onus is felt by them without anyone needing to say anything.'

Apart from learning the correct notes in order to sing accurately, there is also the ownership of presenting the music effectively; that is, understanding what it is you are singing about and being able to communicate that with the audience. The most successful performers are those who sing well and connect with their audience. Much of the success of the Blokes has come from their ability to draw the audience into their performance. For teenage boys this can be a challenge as many find it difficult to express themselves: they don't always have the emotional language that they can use to express how they feel. In some cases, they may not have life experience to draw upon that may assist them in communicating the meaning of the text. It is with these factors in mind that, again, the selection of repertoire is so important. Singing only one style of music or text will not allow the guys to discover the wealth of emotions and stories that can be communicated through song. Apart from the vocal demands of a piece, the emotional demands should be considered and the guys should be challenged by the text. Pearl Shinn Wormhoudt (2001) discusses gender, emotion and singing, and comments:

> Men find it difficult to describe their feelings, which may be one of the deepest reasons the singing man loves to sing. He can allow the composer and the poet to speak (sing) for him and allow his expressive singing to relieve some inhibitions. (p. 113)

The free movement of the body and expression of the face during singing is also something that assists in communicating with the audience and demonstrating a connection between the performer and what they are performing. Again, this is not always easy for the young male performer, as they often feel physically awkward at this time of life. One of the greatest joys in working with the Blokes has been to watch the transformation in the performances given by young men who have moved from being stagnant, lifeless performers to energised performers who look like they enjoy what they do and want the audience to enjoy what they do as well. Another moment of pride is to hear once-tentative ensemble singers audition for solos in front of the whole ensemble.

Further proof of the empowering of young men in the Blokes is that they are looking for gigs for the ensemble to do. They are also developing confidence that they can meet challenges presented to them. It has also recently emerged that some of the members themselves have started directing other male voice choirs in schools. This is an exciting outcome of the group and helps to ensure the further development of male voice singing.

From the Blokes

The achievement of the Blokes since inception has been staggering and exhilarating, but the biggest reward has been to watch, and be a part of, the development of the talents and personalities of the young men who have been involved. The following are accounts from five of the boys who have been involved with the Blokes.

Steve[4]

Steve is one of the original members of the Blokes who attended the first camp, and he has been a member for the past five years. As a child he loved singing but claims that he wasn't very good at it. 'People were always paying me out about my singing and saying that I couldn't really do it. In year seven a teacher told me in front of the class that I was tone deaf and perhaps shouldn't sing so much.' When Steve moved to high school he tried, unsuccessfully, to sing in choirs. He was a good percussionist, and was invited to become a drummer for the Birralee ensembles. Steve was initially hesitant to attend the tenor/bass camp, although he was encouraged to come anyway and try it out. Steve's love for singing was renewed at that camp and he began to learn more about how his voice worked and how to express himself through the music he was singing. He admits that for a while he sang very tentatively, but that now he is confident and happy to sing out. Steve now takes private voice lessons and wants to be the best he can. He also has a desire to make sure that other young men are encouraged, just as he was, to give it a go:

> Since joining the Blokes my confidence has increased, I have learnt to sing and I have created wonderful friendships. I also cannot believe what the group has achieved and the opportunities I have been given. I have travelled overseas to sing at international festivals, I have sung with and for some amazing people as well as giving performances around

>>

Australia. I have learnt so many life skills and become a better musician. Each year I figure I must be too old to keep singing in the Blokes but so far I have kept coming back. Although unable to do music as a career, I love music so much that I won't let anything take it away from me.

Craig

Craig is also an original member of the choir. He joined when he was in his senior year of high school. Craig can remember singing from a very early age. He joined the school choir in Year 2. He sang all through primary school in two fine ensembles that regularly won sections at the Brisbane Eisteddfod. He then moved in Year 5 to a private boys' school, where he continued to sing in several choirs, beginning private singing lessons in Year 6. He was inspired by his choral conductor and sang in various choirs before and after his voice change. Craig recalls the excitement when his choir was placed second in the world in a Trinity College of Music choral exam. He took any opportunity to sing he possibly could, including school musicals, combined schools festivals, school choirs as well as pursuing his voice studies, completing his Grade 7 Trinity College exam. When Craig left school he went to study at the Conservatorium, but left after a year as 'singing had become a job'. Since joining the Blokes, Craig has enjoyed many performances but vividly remembers an early performance given by the Blokes at the Brisbane Eisteddfod. He says:

We sang in the championship section and we did okay but before we went on in the next section we decided it was time to give everything we had and to enjoy ourselves and forget about the competition. We did that and became a different choir in that performance. That performance, while not the first we did as the Blokes, was the one where the Blokes really started. The energy we felt in that performance and the way that we played off each other in performance was exciting and unlike other choral experiences before.

Craig attributes that buzz in performance as a key reason that he is still involved in the Blokes, despite being one of the older guys of the group. He also comments that he has travelled more with the Blokes than he has with his family, and that his involvement in the choir has led him to many people who have become great mates.

The Birralee Blokes is truly a one in a million scenario. The right people, the right time and the right attitude forged a choir that forever changed

>>

the game for young men singing in Australia, and some say the world. The Blokes as a team have kept moving forward through some respected and esteemed choral events, garnering stunning critical acclaim on the world stage.

Mike

Music has been a part of Mike's life for as long as he can remember. He began music classes as a 3-year-old, followed by piano lessons. He progressed through ANZCA and AMEB exams until completing his Associate Diploma in piano in 2007. He learnt oboe and tenor saxophone at high school, and before that, trumpet in primary school. Mike began singing in choirs in Year 2 as a member of a community choir organisation. He sang with them for many years until, in Year 9, his voice changed and he was no longer able to sing treble music. His conductor at the time recommended the Blokes to him. In the past four years, in addition to singing with the Blokes, he has sung in other community ensembles as well as becoming heavily involved in the music program at his school. Mike's commitment to music at his school was rewarded with his appointment as Music Captain and Choral Concertmaster in his senior year. He comments on the biggest differences between singing in other choirs and the Blokes:

> *The difference is the level of ownership the guys have for the choir. While the others have been good, the level of commitment from the members has not been as great and so the drive for professionalism has not been there like it is in the Blokes. All the guys in the Blokes want to be there. They all want to achieve and they all want to have fun. Getting the balance between enjoyment and achievement is tough but crucial to the success for the Blokes. I love being a part of the ensemble and I am so glad that my parents decided I should be involved in music and not cricket so that my Saturday afternoons are spent with my mates singing and socialising and I am not standing out on a cricket field.*

Lewis

A sportsman and a singer, Lewis took the opportunity to attend the tenor/bass camp because his mother said he should. His mother, a music teacher, had insisted that from a young age Lewis should learn music as well as playing rugby league, which he started at 4 years of age. Lewis started as a trumpet player in Year 4, but after two concert-band rehearsals in high school realised that he had no desire to practise

>>

trumpet and so gave up trumpet to sing instead. 'Your voice is with you all the time so there is nothing else to carry around,' he reasoned. He was accepted to a high school on an all-rounder scholarship, which saw him having to contribute to the music program as well as playing rugby for the school and maintaining academic standards. As well as playing for school he played representative rugby for his district and also played touch football and volleyball, and did running, cross-country and swimming. Having dispensed with trumpet he began singing lessons and during Year 9 he successfully auditioned for the school production of *Annie*. Of this experience he noted:

> *I copped some flak from the boys at school about singing but my position as captain of the rugby team meant I didn't get it too tough.*

In Year 10, his voice teacher entered him in the local eisteddfod and the adjudicator awarded him the promising vocalist award. A change to a TAFE college in his senior years allowed him to begin to focus on music and drama, and it was while he was in Year 11 that he attended the tenor/bass camp. Lewis recalls:

> *Attending the camp was daunting because I knew nobody, but I met good guys, had a great time and learnt more about singing in that weekend than I had up till that point. I certainly wanted to be involved in the Blokes and decided that even though I lived five hours drive from Brisbane that I would do all I could to be involved. This meant sometimes wagging college on a Friday afternoon so that I could catch the bus to Brisbane. I would go to rehearsal on Saturday and then catch the bus home again in the evening, arriving home at about 1.30 on Sunday morning.*

Lewis continued to sing with the Blokes for four years and then moved into Resonance of Birralee, a choir for university aged students.

> *I learnt so much in the Blokes about music, choral singing, vocal technique and about myself. Travelling on the bus for that first two years gave me plenty of time to think about what I wanted to do and achieve. I made great mates and had so many opportunities to sing and I loved every moment of it.*

John

John is one Birralee member who fulfils the original motivation for starting the Blokes. He joined the Birralee Juniors as an 8-year-old and enjoyed singing in that choir until in 2000 he began to sing with Birralee Voices as well as they prepared for the trip to Vancouver:

> *The trip to Vancouver was an amazing experience. The choir underwent a huge transition from Westside Youth Choir to Birralee Voices. The difficulty of the music increased and became more diverse and we had to learn how to present the music in a dynamic way. We rose to a new level and the experience got me energised and enthusiastic about singing. We went from singing in shopping centres in Brisbane to singing on the world stage.*

Following the trip to Vancouver, John and his family went to England for three months. John recalls that while away his voice began to change. John continued to sing with the treble choir for two more years, singing lower parts as he lost his upper range. In 2003, John was one of the Birralee boys to try out the tenor/bass experience and for the remainder of that year sang with both the Blokes and Voices choirs. He reflects on the realisation that other teenage boys aren't involved in singing:

> *I was fortunate that the Blokes started just when I needed it to and so I never realised that teenage boys don't sing. Singing with Birralee has been such a key part of my musical training. It has given me great confidence – something to be proud of and something that people appreciated. Through the Blokes, I've gained an appreciation of the power of choral music to touch people across musical styles, languages and cultures because I've had the chance to see it in action.*

In their own words: Reflections on being a Birralee Bloke

Several themes became apparent in the stories of the five members of the ensemble. Many of these were described as social benefits, including comments from other members, such as:

> *I have been able to make great friends with a common interest in music and singing. Also, being in the friendly and open environment that the Blokes provided, helped me to easier traverse that awkward part of life; thus giving me greater social confidence.*
>
> *Meeting different people I wouldn't have met otherwise, mixing with blokes younger and older than me.*

The musical benefits worked in tandem with the social benefits for some members, while others focused purely on the musical experiences:

Making new friends; singing different styles of choral music, and performances when everyone has obviously enjoyed us.

Being in such an original ensemble and having such a renowned reputation in the Australian choral scene in such a short period of time.

Being given the space to grow and mature as singers and musicians.

The group has let me discover an area of music I probably wouldn't have otherwise. Coincidentally I now direct two high school male voice choirs.

My sight reading has improved. I think I have learnt how to interpret the music when I see what Paul does to polish a piece of music.

The experience and benefits of the actual performances and the interaction with audiences featured strongly in many of the Blokes' remarks:

The Blokes give me an alternate way to approach music and an energised performing style. In particular the added energy during performance makes it a far more interesting ensemble to present with.

The Blokes has emboldened me and taught me how to perform charismatically and with vigour to audiences and to enjoy myself while performing. I have lost my fear of the spotlight and thoroughly enjoy performing.

Finding a common passion shared by so many other guys has been awesome and being able to share it with many audiences has been great.

Perhaps, most poignantly, this statement reflects the significance of involvement in the Birralee Blokes for one member:

Singing as part of the Blokes I believe has been a critical factor in my teenage development.

In closing

The journey for the Blokes thus far has been an exciting one, and the ground covered has been substantial for such a short period of time. The degree of musicality that the choir achieves and the dynamic way in which it performs has helped to capture public interest in choral singing. I am immensely proud of who they are and their achievements, and consider myself fortunate to have the opportunity to work with them. There is much more to achieve, but on reflection there have been many factors that have contributed to the success. The following summary of these may be beneficial to others who work with young men. The first is key personnel: a passionate director with a genuine interest in working with young people and a desire to keep challenging themselves and the choristers who sing with them; a musical and chorally aware accompanist who understands the choir and the outcomes they are trying to achieve;

and, finally, support from administrators and/or parents to assist in the general management of the ensemble. Other important factors include:

- Letting the boys be themselves
- Providing regular performance opportunities so that the group and its profile builds
- Knowing how the voice works and what is happening vocally for the choristers
- Choosing music that is appropriate in range, text and musical challenges and that provides variety for the choristers
- Encouraging and empowering the guys to own the ensemble
- Encouraging them to express themselves and give them assistance with this
- Igniting their passion for singing and performing.

And, finally, the last word from Tom, one of the Blokes:

For those who are sceptical, not just of blokes singing but of singing in general, I say to you go and try it out because it could possibly be one of the best things you will ever do!

Endnotes

1   For a discussion on the physiological changes in the male voice, see Cooksey (1999).
2   The positive benefits of competition are noted in Pollack (1999) and Harrison (2005).
3   The pitfalls of the master–apprentice model have recently been researched by Lebler (2007). Similarly, the value of peer teaching in developing generic skills has been noted by Lebler (2007), Green (2001) and Carey and Harrison (2007).
4   Pseudonyms have been used throughout.

References

Adler, A. (2002). A Case Study of Boys' Experiences of Singing in School, unpublished PhD thesis, Toronto, Canada: University of Toronto.

Adler A. & Harrison, S. (2004). Swinging Back the Gender Pendulum: Addressing boys' needs in music education, research and practice, in L. Bartel (ed.) *Research to Practice: A biennial series – Questioning the music education paradigm*, pp. 270–89, Toronto, Canada: Canadian Music Educators Association.

Barham, T.J & Nelson D.L. (1991). *The Boy's Changing Voice – New solutions for today's choral teacher*, United States: Belwyn Mills Publishing.

Beall, A.E. & Sternberg, R.J. (1993). *The Psychology of Gender*, New York: Guilford Press.

Carey, G. & Harrison, S.D. (2007). The Practice of Pedagogy, paper presented at the NACTMUS National Conference, Brisbane http://www.nactmus.org.au/papers01/confpapers.html, accessed 5/02/2007.

Cooksey, J. (1999). *Working with Adolescent Voices*, St Louis, MO: Concordia Publishing House.

Eagly, A.H. & Steffen, V.J. (1984). Gender Stereotypes Stem from the Distribution of Women and Men into Social Roles, *Journal of Personality and Social Psychology, 46*, pp. 735–54, reproduced in C. Stangor (ed.), *Stereotypes and Prejudice: Essential readings*, pp. 142–60, Philadelphia: Psychology Press.

Green, L. (2001). *How Popular Musicians Learn: A way ahead for music education*, Aldershot: Ashgate.

Harrison, S.D. (2001). Real Men Don't Sing, *Australian Voice, 7*, pp. 31–6.

Harrison, S.D. (2005). Music and Sport: New approaches to scoring, *Australian Journal for Music Education, 1*, pp. 56–61.

Lebler, D. (2007). Student-As-Master? Reflections on a learning innovation in popular music pedagogy, *International Journal of Music Education*, 25(3), pp. 205–21.

Maccoby, E.E. (ed.) (1966). *The Development of Sex Differences*, Stanford: Stanford University Press.

Phillips, K. (2003). Creating a Safe Environment for Singing, *Choral Journal*, 43(10), pp. 41–43.

Pollack, W. (1999), *Real Boys*, New York: Holt.

Shinn Wormhoudt, P. (2001). *With a Song in My Psyche: On the psychology of singing and teaching singing*, United States: Xlibris Corporation.

Susman, E., Feagans, L. & Ray, W. (1992). *Emotion, Cognition, Health and Development in Children and Adolescents*, Hillsdale, NJ: Erlbaum.

12 | The Ten Tenors: Mateship through music

MATTHEW HICKEY, Executive Producer, The Ten Tenors

In 2008, The Ten Tenors celebrated its 10th anniversary as a full-time ensemble. Assembled as a musical gag for a corporate performance, The Ten Tenors have gone on to become one of Australia's most successful musical exports, with its official biography listing a large number of career achievements: the release of six albums (including one recorded at London's famed Abbey Road studio) and three live concert DVDs; more than 1500 live concerts throughout 18 countries and on six continents; and sampling over 70 different types of international beer and having ordered them in eight different languages. The final entry in that list, included obviously for comedic value, provides clear insight into the motto that has always underpinned the group's development: let's take our jobs seriously, but let's not take ourselves too seriously.

Through my more than 10 years of involvement as both a performer and as Director of The Ten Tenors, I have shared in the amazing experiences and success that membership of this unique organisation has afforded us. Within this chapter I seek only to provide an abridged glimpse into what has been a story of amazingly good fortune, good times and most importantly of all, incredible friendship born out of a bunch of men making music together. These scattered reflections on our journey together seek only to serve as an encouragement to other young men to make music, ideally together. To the extent that the following pages are historically inaccurate, viewed through the rose-tinted lenses of hindsight, or somewhat embellished with poor attempts at humour for literary effect, I accept full responsibility, safe in the knowledge that my merciless colleagues will hold me to account, somehow!

Early days

In 1995, The Ten Tenors gathered together to perform at a corporate function in its home town, Brisbane. During the 1990s, The Three Tenors: Carreras, Domingo and Pavarotti, were at the height of their ascendancy, having sparked the interest of a new generation, and perhaps a new audience, with their spectacular performance at the Baths of Caracalla in Rome on the eve of the 1990 FIFA World Cup. Inspired by this, when Channel Ten Brisbane engaged social commentator and raconteur Ken Lord to produce entertainment for the company's Anniversary Birthday Ball, the idea to assemble *10 tenors* for Channel *Ten*'s birthday, no doubt, appeared to be inspired.

Outstanding Brisbane opera singer Jason Barry-Smith (a baritone, ironically enough) was responsible for recruiting and training the singers (rumour has it that at least one of the original 10 wasn't a tenor) in their initial three-song repertoire of: 'Funiculi, Funicula', 'Nessun Dorma' and 'You Stepped Out of a Dream' (the original Channel Ten theme song). The Ten Tenors was a hit with the audience, and the tenors themselves thought the audience, many of whom were likely to have felt a little under the weather the next day (to put it euphemistically), were a welcome change from the usually genteel opera audiences they were accustomed to.

Throughout the following few years, The Ten Tenors made occasional performances at corporate events (again, generally late in the evenings to audiences well on their way towards next-day hangovers) and singing the national anthem at sporting events (at the invitation of teams who, in nearly every case, subsequently lost on the day) while working towards completion of university studies in music. By 1998, graduation was imminent for most of us and, with professional opera opportunities in Australia, much less Queensland, limited, unemployment looked a very real prospect. Suddenly, what had privately been viewed by the tenors, and probably many of those around us, as a bit of a scam, seemed like a sensible interim activity while we waited for the 'real' opportunities to present themselves. It wouldn't be long before many of us realised we'd *found* the real opportunity, but it would be years before our activities in The Ten Tenors were viewed with any sort of legitimacy by many of our contemporaries.

We thought we'd struck gold one evening when we heard that a local restaurant had been booked by a conference of theatre managers from all around Queensland and New South Wales. We'd always joked about arriving en masse in some public place and launching into song, just to see the reaction it provoked. Kamikaze-style we called it;

undergraduate humour, obviously, but then we *were* all undergraduates. Realising this could finally be our moment to simultaneously realise the kamikaze fantasy and secure ourselves some work, we descended upon the restaurant, unloading an electric keyboard from the boot of a car we parked in the tow-away zone out front, plugging it into the nearest power outlet and launching into our routine quickly, presuming we'd be asked to leave any minute. Fortunately for us, the theatre managers thought the restaurant had arranged our performance (many of them probably still do) and the restaurant manager thought his patrons had hired us, so we managed to complete our full set without interruption. Business cards were being proffered from left and right, and by the end of the week we had offers for our first tour of full-length theatrical shows.

Despite having secured a paying tour, we didn't actually have enough repertoire to sustain a full show, so the following few months were spent furiously arranging and learning new songs, developing some on-stage patter and hoping for the best. This 'necessity being the mother of invention' approach came to typify The Ten Tenors' artistic development over the coming years, and our inimitable ad hoc style can largely be attributed to these early experiences. By the end of 1998, we had performed our first tour, engaged management, recorded our first album and committed to the ensemble full-time by quitting our day jobs and hitting the road in earnest.

Over the following three years, The Ten Tenors performed throughout the length and breadth of Australia. From large venues in tiny outback towns to tiny venues in capital cities, we built our fan base, gig by gig, operating under the premise that we'd pretty much accept any gig that was offered to us. Through countless kilometres travelled in the back of mini-vans, and even more countless hours sitting around backstage, waiting for gigs to happen, an intense camaraderie developed and, simultaneously but hardly surprisingly, our work as musicians began to improve, too.

By the middle of 2001, we had toured almost to the point of exhausting our market. The great 'crossover' fascination, which was seen as the saviour of the classical genre, was yet to take hold for record companies. Without major label record company support and despite the success we were enjoying in regional Australia, we struggled to gain the attention of audiences in the big cities, which we so desperately required if we were to remain viable. The writing was on the wall, and although none of us dared speak it out loud at the time, we've all reflected after the fact that we felt our days were numbered when we were thrown a lifeline from the most unlikely of places: Germany.

Don't mention the war!

As young opera students, we'd all been conditioned to view Europe as the 'promised land' for opera singers. As individuals we aspired to go there, and were probably all privately convinced we'd end up there some way or another, but I'm sure *none* of us ever imagined it would be The Ten Tenors that would take us there. A friend of the group who had studied with us at university happened to be studying in Berlin. One evening while in the audience at *Bar Jeder Vernunft*, arguably Berlin's premiere cabaret venue, she courageously and without our knowledge approached the proprietor and informed them she knew of an act that would bring the house down there. After a period of initial discussions, we'd heard nothing and, of course, presumed the Germans had realised we were as terrible as all our opera mates seemed to think we were. Our fears were unfounded, though; shortly thereafter, *Bar Jeder Vernunft*, in partnership with a sister venue the *Fliegende Bauten* in Hamburg, offered The Ten Tenors a contract to appear six nights per week for a month in each of the venues. It was, without question, the turning point in our careers.

As the date approached we were conflicted about how and what we should perform. It had never really occurred to us that we might be viewed as a cabaret act; we were never really quite sure how to define what our act was (sometimes it's still a problem). So much of our on-stage shtick was (and still is) predicated on in-jokes, double entendres and clever use of English. It had been the thing we thought carried our show, since most people 'in the know' were of the opinion that we weren't much chop, musically. How would we fare against a 'sophisticated, European audience' when the only thing we had to rely on, our gags, might not be understood?

In response to this, many well-meaning friends and colleagues flooded us with 'tips' and 'advice' for our forthcoming performances – sing this, don't sing that; do this, don't do that; say this, don't say that; and whatever you do, don't mention the war! (Seriously, I don't know how many times we heard that last one.) In the end, acknowledging that if we were to fail in front of these audiences then at least we'd have failed doing our thing, we resolved to perform the show exactly as we'd done in those countless outback town halls and RSL clubs across Australia for the previous three years.

The European audience was every bit as sophisticated as we'd feared. They were so sophisticated that they spoke English well enough to understand nearly all of our jokes as well as, if not better than, our audiences had at home. As we finished the show, the audience gave us a standing ovation, and chanted for an encore. Having no real yardstick to measure against as far as German audiences were concerned, we presumed this was a good sign and hoped for the best. We knew they hadn't booed us off the stage, and that was good enough for us.

The reviews in the Berlin newspapers sealed our fate. Within days, the entire season was a sell-out and The Ten Tenors were the talk of the town. We had become the latest 'must see', almost without realising it and certainly without intending to. The season in Hamburg the following month was even more successful than Berlin, as word spread. Major record labels and concert promoters invited us for meetings in expensive restaurants and we began to realise that, where only months before we thought we were finished, suddenly we were actually just getting started.

What we hadn't considered in our terror-filled contemplation of the 'European audience' in the months leading up to our debut performance before them was that the audience we should have feared most was the one we'd already been playing to for years. Audiences in regional Australia are grateful for live performances, but our experience was they didn't clap at (much less cheer or stand for) us if we weren't any good. In response, we'd honed our material town after town after town until we could rely on the fact that the audiences would laugh and clap and, occasionally cheer for more. We credit our international success generally to the trials by silence we were put through by Australian audiences in the years before we ever got the opportunity to take our act offshore, when we were simply not that good. (The tenors still laugh about one performance, in a town that shall remain nameless, when all that could be heard at the end of each song was the woman in the second row's knitting needles clacking together. Happy days!)

What have we learned about making music as Australian men?

Throughout the years that have followed our initial breakout success in Berlin and Hamburg, we've added regular touring routes throughout many other European nations, the United States, South Africa and Asia, and have continued to tour Australia as often as possible. Wherever we go, no matter what part of the world, inevitably the most frequent thing we hear from audience is 'it looks like you're having fun' followed closely by 'it seems like you all really enjoy each other's company'. It's pleasing to us that audiences recognise these two elements, irrespective of where we are in the world, since they are, largely, the reason we have continued to exist as an ensemble.

If there is any secret to what we've done, musically, and the way we've managed to capture our audience's imagination with it, I'm absolutely certain it's because what the audience perceives is true: it *is* fun and we *do* enjoy each other's company. You can't fake that – it's either true or it isn't, and people *know* the difference. I believe it is part of the human condition to desire pleasure and genuine human relationships, and to be able to recognise these in others who are enjoying the two. Throughout our history as a group, there have been times when our existence made no sense, artistically or financially, but in spite of that we just kept on keeping on, not always because we thought that some great golden success was just over the horizon, but because, more than anything else, it was fun and we enjoyed each other's company. It still is and we still do.

Through the discussions I've had with members of our group, I've learned that their experiences as young male musicians were as varied as they are. For some, their youthful music making was as natural to them as breathing, and they recalled or encountered no peer or parental resistance or discouragement of their musicianship, while for others the wounds of schoolyard taunts were still ringing in their ears as they described them to me. In any case, the common elements that led them beyond adolescent music making and into professional careers as musicians was that there was the presence of *some* kindly, supportive person who believed in them (whether parent, grandparent, teacher, aunt, uncle, friend) and an environment for making music (whether school, church, choral society, orchestra, amateur musical society), which provided positive experiences that far outweighed the negative experiences their involvement in music may have provoked elsewhere.

The pages of this book are filled with the thoughts and ideas of those kinds of people; we're humbled to be here alongside them. As an ensemble, I suppose, The Ten Tenors represents the professional success that can result for young men who get involved with music, but I hope this chapter conveys that the real success we've all shared is the strongest bonds of friendship – genuine human relationships with each other and the sheer fun that making music can bring. In the end, isn't that the whole point, of music and life?